THE ANTIQUES BOOK OF
VICTORIAN INTERIORS

THE ANTIQUES BOOK OF
VICTORIAN INTERIORS

COMPILED BY ELISABETH DONAGHY GARRETT

Crown Publishers, Inc., New York

Contents

Introduction

> To us, our house was not unsentient matter—it had a heart, and a soul, and eyes to see us with; and approvals and solicitudes, and deep sympathies; it was of us, and we were in its confidence, and lived in its grace and in the peace of its benediction. We never came home from an absence that its face did not light up and speak out its eloquent welcome—and we could not enter it unmoved.

Thus Mark Twain evoked his beloved Hartford, Connecticut, home (see pp. 86-93). For many other Americans in the second half of the nineteenth century, the home was an animated presence. The home and its inhabitants were mirror images; one reflected the other, penning the outlines and filling in the shading of this double portrait. Andrew Jackson Downing in his influential *The Architecture of Country Houses* (1850), wrote: "How often does the interior of the same house convey to us a totally different impression, when inhabited and furnished by different families." Also at the outset of the second half of the nineteenth century, Samuel Sloan, the Philadelphia author of several books on domestic architecture, pronounced: "A man's dwelling at the present day, is not only an index of his wealth, but also of his character. The moment he begins to build, his tact for arrangement, his private feelings, the refinement of his taste and the peculiarities of his judgment are all laid bare for public inspection and criticism." The celebrated American proponent of the English Reform Movement, Clarence Cook, in his *The House Beautiful* (1878), was still advising in the third quarter of the nineteenth century that the living-room "ought to represent the culture of the family,—what is their taste, what feeling they have for art; it should represent themselves." The Victorian home should, then, above all things manifest individuality. The underlying import of the ever-accelerating accumulation of accessories and collections throughout the second half of the nineteenth century was their role in clarifying the character of the homemaker. Sarah Josepha Hale observed in her *Manners; or, Happy Homes and Good Society All The Year Round* (1868): "Character, it has well been said, is seen through small openings, and certainly is as clearly displayed in the arrangements and adornments of a house as in any other way. Who cannot read grace, delicacy, and refinement in the lady of a house, simply by looking at the little elegances and beauties with which she has surrounded herself in her home? . . . As home is the place where our best and happiest hours are passed, nothing which will beautify or adorn it can be of trifling importance." The Victorian emphasis on accessories and collections is richly illustrated in Frederick Church's Olana (pp. 74-85), Mark Twain's Hartford home, George Sealy's The Open Gates (pp. 104-110), George Vanderbilt's Biltmore (pp. 111-123) and William Wetmore's Chateau-sur-Mer (pp. 124-129).

This proliferation of ornament meant that the shelf assumed a place of unparalleled importance in Victorian interior architecture and furniture design. Whereas mantelshelves had usually remained starkly bare in the colonial home—"as there was not an ornament in the house the mantel was unadorned; even the candle-sticks would have been thought superfluous"—by the third quarter of the nineteenth century the mantelshelf was frequently double-tiered and furniture was multishelved for display (as the buffet in George Sealy's dining room, p. 107). Nathalie Dana recalled the mantelshelf in the library of her late nineteenth-century Eastlake-inspired Lenox Hill home: "The passion for bric-a-brac reached its climax around the fireplace. Incorporated in the woodwork over the mantelshelf was the Milton shield especially made in silver by Tiffany & Co. . . . Around the shield were shelves in fancy shapes supported by gracefully turned spindles. The ornaments on these shelves ranged from marble copies of Forum columns to a wasp's nest suspended by a yellow ribbon from a finial shaped like a flame. Later this place was taken over by a sea-porcupine with spikes and bulging eyes which had been brought by hand from the Pacific coast. A bronze clock ticking on the mantelshelf gave a homelike touch, and below it a flight of birds was realistically represented on a row of tiles." The omnipresence of the shelf in the Victorian home is well illustrated in Harriet Spofford's *Art Decoration Applied to Furniture* (1878), where under furniture suitable for the drawing room she lists, in addition to tables, "an Easel, an Étagère, Corner shelves, Tall cabinet for curios, relics, minerals, etc.—the main piece of furniture in the room, and a Hanging cabinet."

In addition to lending an individuality to the home and providing a character portrait of the owner, accessories were meant to educate, and the didactic demands on the Victorian home weighed heavily. The selection of a vase for the mantel or a print for the wall was of momentous concern to the future of the household young. "I look upon this living-room as an important agent in the education of life;" wrote Clarence Cook, "it will make a great difference to the children who grow up in it, and to all whose experience is associated with it, whether it be a beautiful and cheerful room, or a homely and bare one. . . . It is no trifling matter, whether we select a fine [object] or a second-rate one."

The Victorian household was viewed as a schoolroom of virtue. "Our hope is not in schools," the Reverend Matthew Hale Smith advised, "but in the home. . . ." The Victorian home was perceived as a haven from the world—a sacred place, a walled garden, fashioned and fortified to protect children against the harsh realities of a complex machine age. From an earlier role as adjunct, mother became the dominant figure of the family, creating with her strength, devotion, piety, and knowledge a cult of domesticity, the ambience within which proper nurture could proceed. "When our land is filled with virtuous and patriotic mothers," the Reverend John S.C. Abbott proclaimed in his widely-read *The Mother at Home* (1834), "then will it be filled with virtuous and patriotic men." The pervasive and soothing presence of the mother in the Victorian home is evident in Andrew Jackson Downing's advice on furniture for the parlor: "A great variety of light and fanciful tables is produced by the French furniture makers. They are not only useful in the drawing-room for books, ladies' work, flower-baskets, etc., but they give an air of feminine taste and occupation to an apartment, without which it is apt to look stiff and solemn." In a time when, according to Catherine Beecher, who wrote a series of instruction manuals for this new American woman, "Everything is moving and changing," the home is pictured as providing solid, stable virtues and a respite from the frequently-confusing, ever-accelerating and multifaceted Victorian world. Yet the home does very much reflect the confusion, acceleration, and multifaceted aspect of the outside world.

The Industrial Revolution introduced the consumer to the element of choice—something which had not been available to the colonial consumer. The Victorian enjoyed both a choice of style and of quantity. He was, in fact, bombarded by a rapidly-changing profusion of styles and confusion of ornament. In their quest for the picturesque, Victorians set out to adapt the art of other places in other times to their own comfort. Books, world's fairs, and travel facilitated this pursuit. From the uncluttered simplicity of the Greek Revival style as seen in the Marshall-Hixon House (pp. 13-16), the Sam Davis Home (pp. 40-47), and the John Wornall House (pp. 66-73), to the Italianate suggestions of Ashland (pp. 17-21), to the Grecian, Italianate and Gothic union at San Francisco (pp. 56-65), on to the Persian exoticism of Olana and George Sealy's salmagundi of styles at The Open Gates, we see the Victorian quest for novelty.

The accelerated pace of life outside the home wove itself into the fabric of the home as well. Generations-old furniture was not admired by most Victorians. In fact, one home owner could ask, "What is life without new furniture?" And Max O'Rell who visited Grand Rapids on April 24, 1890, could report: "Grand Rapids is noted for its furniture manufactories. . . .I was not very surprised to hear that when the various retail houses come to make their yearly selections, they will not look at any models of the previous season, so great is the rage for novelties in every branch of industry in this novelty-looking America . . .Over in Europe, furniture is reckoned by periods. Here it is an affair of seasons. Very funny to have to order a new sideboard or wardrobe, 'to be sent home without delay' for fear of its being out of date."

This acceleration is also reflected in the interior by a move away from the homogeneity, regularity, clarity, and neatness which characterized the colonial home. Homogeneity was not an attribute of the Victorian home. Rooms were decorated in a flash of fabrics and styles. By the 1870s cozy corners and nooks further dissipated any sense of cohesion in the parlor and screens promoted this diversity and faceting of the Victorian interior.

It is this faceting which also characterizes the Victorian home: a faceting brought about by considering the room in multiples rather than as a unit, and by the profusion of ornament, the profusion of furniture, the profusion of textiles. Upholstered furniture "deep and luxurious" and "in profusion" abounded, and carpets—once laid in a wall-to-wall regularity—now lay scattered and layered in plenty while windows, tables, doorways, mantels, picture frames, looking glasses, and even lamps were frequently swathed and swagged in a flurry of fabric. Anne Ellis recalled the fabric niceties which in the 1890s she had planned for her home at the Bonanza Mine in Colorado: "These are the first things I fix for my future home and life: little bags of pieces of silk—those I had seen had bangles on the bottom; I had no bangles, but made some by boring holes in pennies and sewing these on. These bags of different colors were quite the thing to hang from the corner of a picture; little balls made of milkweed silk, colored, and tied with baby ribbon, were supposed to be very effective for this, too. If you didn't have a 'throw' over the right-hand corner of each picture, well—you just weren't in it, that's all. Throws were used, too, on the corners of stands, letting the long-fringed or hand-painted ends hang down. It would be held in place either by a shell, a specimen, or a piece of glass brought from the World's Fair with a picture of one of the buildings on it. In addition to the little bags, I made a crazy work lambrequin."

Sculpture, plants, paintings, prints, ceramics, peacock feathers, and weapons crowded in upon this abundance, providing in each case, as can be seen through the illustrations in this volume, an air of individuality to each room and a character study of its creator.

In 1850 Andrew Jackson Downing pronounced: "We believe above all things under heaven, in the power and virtue of the individual home. We devote our life and humble efforts to raising its condition." It is this determined dedication to the power and virtue of the home which we celebrate in *The Antiques Book of Victorian Interiors.*

THE ANTIQUES BOOK OF

VICTORIAN INTERIORS

The Marshall-Hixon house in Mobile

BY MARGARET ROSE INGATE

BENJAMIN FRANKLIN MARSHALL was born in Camden, South Carolina, in 1810 and came to Mobile in 1829, where he grew wealthy as a cotton factor. When he started to build his house in Spring Hill (now part of Mobile) in 1852, he was one of only a few residents of the

Fig. 1. The mahogany block-front secretary with bonnet top in the entrance hall of the Marshall-Hixon house was purchased from a John Howland by Mrs. Hixon's great-grandfather Calvin Pardee about 1850. It is thought to be of Rhode Island origin, 1750-1760. Opposite it is a richly inlaid mahogany Federal card table of 1790-1800. The American Victorian chairs flanking the table were made between 1835 and 1850. Above the card table hangs a pastel portrait of Ariovistus Pardee (1778-1853) painted in 1804 by an unknown artist. The sitter was the grandfather of Calvin Pardee. Beyond the louvered doors is an eighteenth-century tall-case clock made by a Dutch clockmaker in New York. The chandeliers, which date from about 1850, were originally in a neighboring house, but were installed here before the McMillans bought the house. The carpet in the foreground is a Turkoman, the small one beyond it, a Caucasian prayer rug. The dentils and cornices here and throughout the interior are molded of plaster reinforced with horsehair. *Except as noted, photographs are by Helga Photo Studio.*

Fig. 2. The living room is dominated by what is believed to be a French overmantel looking glass in a baroque gilded frame. It was imported for the house during the Marshall family's residence. The late nineteenth-century lacquered and painted tilt-top table in the corner beside the fireplace, the card table with banjo pedestal of c. 1840, and the Queen Anne candlestand with bird-cage support and snake feet of c. 1760 descended in the McMillan and Hixon families. The teapot on the card table is yellow-glazed earthenware decorated with pink strawberries and green leaves. The portrait of Lucia Weimer (a cousin of Mrs. Hixon's mother) above the card table was painted about 1880 on doeskin, and is signed *Phillips*. The small mahogany side chair beside the candlestand dates from about 1840. The deep-crimson rug is Turkish. The chandeliers in the living room and the adjoining dining room are Waterford crystal.

city who chose to live year round any distance from the fashionable district along and near Government Street. Spring Hill, more than two hundred feet above sea level, had become a popular summer retreat from the torrid heat and mosquitoes which were thought to cause the major epidemics of yellow fever that swept the low-lying city center from the early eighteenth into the nineteenth century. Few families lived there year round, however.[1] For years the only public transportation to Spring Hill was by mule-drawn trolley. Old Shell Road, paralleling the trolley route, was opened in 1851.

Marshall selected a site identified in the town plan of 1828 as square 19 on which to build his house.[2] It was part of a one-square-mile Spanish land grant that was later divided. T-shape in plan, the house was completed in 1853 (see Fig. 4). The exterior is unbled cypress, and the original cedar shutters are still in place. Broad steps, the treads covered with slate, lead to a Greek revival porch with Doric columns. The double doors of the main entrance open into a wide hall which extends almost the full depth of the house, giving onto a transverse hall that leads to the wings. The entrance hall is divided at the

Fig. 3. The comfortable and functional library is lighted by windows framed with Egyptian revival surrounds similar to the doorframes in the hall. Bookcases (two are partly visible in the mirror) and the door surround repeat the Egyptian revival framing. The Oriental bronze vessels on the hearth and the bronze dragon beside the chair at the right were part of Calvin Pardee's collection of bronzes dating from the Ming period through the eighteenth century. The major portion of the collection was given to the Metropolitan Museum. The prayer rug before the hearth is Turkish.

middle by louvered doors set in a massive Egyptian revival surround (see Fig. 1). The front doors and matching double back doors are similarly framed. The living room and dining room are at the left of the hall. What was originally a double parlor at the right of the hall is now a library and a bedroom.

In the center of the circular drive in front of the house is a large brick fountain built by the Marshalls. A carriage house is located behind the house. An unusual feature of the property is a forty-foot-deep cistern with a beautifully vaulted brick ceiling located underground near the back door to the house.

Benjamin Marshall, financially ruined by the Civil War, sold the house and property in 1863 to the son of

Don Miguel Eslava, who had been treasurer and customs collector in Mobile during the Spanish occupation. The Eslava family sold it in 1908 to Thomas Byrne, a benefactor of Spring Hill College, who sold it to the Reverend and Mrs. Leighton McMillan in 1931. The McMillans extensively restored the house, carefully preserving the integrity of the architectural plan and the interior. Many of the furnishings in the house today are McMillan family pieces. The house is presently owned by the McMillans' daughter and son-in-law, Mr. and Mrs. Carl Hixon, who have made minor alterations to it to accommodate their four children.

[1] Notable exceptions were William A. Dawson, who started Yesterhouse (now known as Carolina Hall in Spring Hill in 1832 and his brother John C. Dawson, who built Palmetto Hall there in 1846 (see ANTIQUES for March 1964, p. 300, Fig. 12). The Gaillard house (see ANTIQUES for March 1964, p. 296, Fig. 3) was built in the 1830's in Spring Hill, and Roger Stewart's Stewartfield in 1845 (see ANTIQUES for March 1964, p. 301, Fig. 14). Spring Hill College was established in Spring Hill in 1830.

[2] The property once belonged to Bishop Michael Portier, the first Roman Catholic bishop of West Florida and Alabama. In 1823 a wooden church and graveyard occupied the site of the present house.

Fig. 4. This aerial view of the Marshall-Hixon property taken in 1951 clearly shows the T-shape plan of the house. The brick fountain in front of the house is hidden by the magnolia and oak trees. *Photograph by Roy Thigpen.*

Ashland

BY THOMAS D. CLARK

THE FAMOUS Kentucky statesman Henry Clay (1777–1852) bought Ashland farm outside Lexington in 1811 from the estate of the patriarch of Kentucky government, George Nicholas (1754?–1799). The house stood on a tract of 235 fertile acres which, in time, Clay more than doubled in size by judicious purchases of neighboring land.

To enlarge the house Clay called on Benjamin Henry Latrobe, who wrote him in August and early September 1813 that he had made preliminary drawings for two wings.[1] As speaker of the United States House of Representatives, Clay was then much preoccupied with the War of 1812, and Latrobe had difficulty getting him to supply the dimensions of the existing house at Ashland. Only in January 1814 did Clay decide to begin building at least the north wing of the house. Clay drove a shrewd bargain with the builder, John Fisher Jr., who estimated the cost of the job at $695.89. This was to be paid in three installments—$345.89 in cash immediately, $200 worth of horses, and $150 in cash less Clay's payments of 7/6 a day to each laborer. In addition, Clay promised the workmen board and two meals a day "of plain substantial dieting." The finished wing was insured on July 6, 1814, for $2,000 of its estimated value of $2,500.[2]

Pl. I. Ashland, built 1853–1857 for James B. Clay (d. 1864) from plans drawn by Thomas Lewinski (c. 1802–1882). The house is built on the site, and perhaps on much of the foundation, of the house that James Clay's father, Henry Clay, bought in 1811. *Photographs are by Helga Photo Studio.*

Before the wing was completed Clay was sent to Ghent by President James Madison, as a member of the commission that was to draw up a peace treaty with England. From there he went to Paris, where for 660 francs he bought a silver coffeepot and possibly several cases of porcelain. By March 25, 1815, he had crossed to London, where he made arrangements to have his French purchases shipped home from Liverpool on the United States vessel *Neptune*. While in England Clay spent considerable time at cattle shows buying breeding stock to raise on the fertile bluegrass at Ashland.

In addition to stock farming, Clay produced hemp, grains, and tobacco at Ashland. And when the house was completed he added a large barn, an overseer's house, an impressive brick privy, a carriage house, a smokehouse, an icehouse (see Fig. 1), and a dairy cooling pit.

The present house (Pl. I) was built between 1853 and 1857 by Clay's son James, who bought the estate at a public sale in September 1853 for $45,408.12.

Pl. II. The arched doorway leading to the drawing room is made of ash cut on the estate. According to family tradition Henry Clay bought the draperies in Lyons, France, in 1814. The campaign banner on the wall between the draperies is from the hotly contested presidential campaign of 1844, when Clay unsuccessfully opposed James Knox Polk. The silver urn in front of it was presented to Henry Clay by the goldsmiths and silversmiths of New York City in 1845. (An article about the urn appeared in ANTIQUES for July 1977, p. 112.)

Pl. III. The window and door surrounds, baseboards, and the door of this sitting room are made from ash cut on the estate. The table and Bohemian glass wine decanter and glasses belonged to Henry Clay. The other furnishings and paintings date from the occupancy of James B. Clay and Henry Clay McDowell.

Pl. IV. The dining room is one of the most charming rooms in the house. The portrait of Henry Clay over the mantel is signed *Franconia,* and those of his wife, Lucretia Hart Clay, and Julia Pratt Clay, a daughter-in-law, are by Oliver Frazer (1808–1864). On the mantel nineteenth-century French porcelain vases flank a bowl that once belonged to Henry Clay. The velvet draperies hung in Henry Clay's house at Ashland. The Honduras mahogany dining and drop-leaf tables are said to have been brought to Kentucky from Virginia. The silver service on the drop-leaf table bears inscriptions tracing Henry Clay's career. It was a wedding present to his granddaughter Ann Clay from Dr. Charles H. Mercer of New Orleans. The silver pitcher on the drop-leaf table was presented to Henry Clay by the Association of Mechanics and Workmen of Washington, D. C., in 1832. The lace runner was embroidered in 1820 by a group of women in Ireland for Mrs. Clay. Worked in both ends are twenty-three stars symbolizing the states in the Union at the time.

Pl. V. This bedroom, known as the Clay bedroom, contains Henry Clay's high-post bed of mahogany and mahogany veneer. The silk patchwork quilt was made during the presidential campaign of 1844 by the Whig ladies of Philadelphia, who gave it to Clay. The battered deerskin trunk accompanied Clay on stagecoaches and steamboats as he traveled to and from Washington. The blue glass lamp and the washstand, pitcher, and bowl are McDowell family pieces.

Pl. VI. The bed and the looking-glass frame were made especially for this upstairs bedroom from ash cut on the estate. A late nineteenth-century ingrain carpet covers the floor.

He then immediately tore down the existing house, selling parts to souvenir makers. He specified that the proceeds should be used for charitable purposes, but the destruction of the house created a furor among Henry Clay's admirers. One of them, George D. Prentice, the Whig editor of the Louisville *Daily Journal*, almost challenged James to a duel.

The new house was designed by Thomas Lewinski and was built on what may be the foundations of the old one. However, James Clay did not enjoy it for long. An ardent sympathizer with the Southern cause during the Civil War, he died in Montreal, a political exile, in 1864. The following year his widow, Susannah Jacob Clay, sold the estate for $90,000 to John B. Bowman (1824–1891), regent of the newly created Kentucky Agricultural and Mechanical College. When that venture failed, Kentucky University, of which the college was then a part, sold Ashland in 1882 to Major Henry Clay McDowell, the husband of Henry Clay Jr.'s daughter Ann. McDowell made many improvements to the house and farm.

By 1950 most of the farm had been broken up into housing lots, while the house and the twenty acres immediately around it were transferred to the Henry Clay Memorial Foundation by Nanette McDowell, a daughter-in-law of Henry Clay McDowell. At that time much of the Clay and McDowell family furniture was donated to the foundation. Since then many other objects associated with Henry Clay have found their way back to Ashland.

On May 9, 1825, while Henry Clay was secretary of state, he wrote to his brother-in-law James Brown (1766–1835), then minister to France, asking if it might not be possible to buy furniture and other household furnishings in France for less than they could be bought in the United States. Clay stated that he planned to rent a house in Washington in July and needed to economize.[3]

In June, Brown volunteered to act as purchasing agent and reported that clocks, looking glasses, candelabra, porcelain, and silver-gilt wares could be bought advantageously in France, while England was better for silver plate. Indian damask equaled French silk for curtains and upholstery but was cheaper, while French carpets, although expensive, were superior to British carpets. Brown added that American mahogany furniture was better and less expensive than its European counterparts.

In September Lucretia Clay sent her sister Anne Hart Brown a list of things she wanted her to buy for her—a list which unfortunately has not survived. And in the same month Clay wrote to James Brown: "I am glad to be able to tell you that I have continued to feel the most sensible benefit from the system of economy and exertion which I adopted to get out of my pecuniary difficulties."

On October 13 James reported that everything was in hand except the looking glasses. However, he told Clay that he was welcome to take the looking glasses from the Browns' Lexington house. James warned that it was much harder to shop in Paris than Americans imagined: "You may be grossly imposed upon in the articles as well as the prices and therefore much care and attention are necessary. . . ."

The shipment for Clay left Paris for Cherbourg on November 12, 1825, and was loaded on the *Montano*, which left France on November 25. Clay's goods were consigned to Isaac Bell, a New York merchant. Brown

Pl. VII. Henry Clay had the spool crib to the left of the bed made for his grandchildren during the 1840's. The fire screen and conversation chair were once owned by Clay. The other furnishings date from the occupancy of James B. Clay and Major Henry Clay McDowell. The wallpaper was designed especially for this room, but the lace curtains are a recent acquisition.

sent Clay a manifest detailing the contents of the shipment and the prices paid. Although the manifest has vanished, letters reveal that the shipment included an "envelope" of trimmed cloth, no doubt a package of draperies.

In addition to the family furnishings illustrated here, the collection at Ashland today includes a hatbox, dress coat, and green dressing gown that belonged to Henry Clay, a red velvet gown owned by Lucretia, an elaborate mother-of-pearl model of Ash-

land presented to Henry Clay's family by New York admirers in 1852, and a carriage given to Henry Clay by Newark, New Jersey, supporters in 1833 which he used until his death.

[1] James F. Hopkins and Mary Wilma Hargreaves, eds., *The Papers of Henry Clay* (University Press of Kentucky, Lexington), vol. 1 (1961), pp. 599-600, 818-819, 820.

[2] *Ibid.*, vol. 1, pp. 950-951.

[3] *Ibid.*, vol. 4 (1972), p. 336.

Fig. 1. The first of these two icehouses was built in the early 1820's and the second, which is connected to it, soon thereafter. The brick-lined pits, ten feet in diameter and sixteen feet deep, were used to store large quantities of pond ice packed in sawdust for family use during summer. The runoff was diverted to cool milk and butter from the farm's dairy.

The Theodore Roosevelt Birthplace in New York City

BY DAVID M. KAHN

THEODORE ROOSEVELT was born in 1858 in the brownstone row house at number 28 East Twentieth Street in New York City. The row of houses had been built ten years earlier on speculation, and Roosevelt's grandfather Cornelius Roosevelt had bought both number 28 and the adjoining house, number 26, as wedding presents for two of his sons, Theodore Sr. and Robert. Theodore Sr. moved into number 28 in 1854 with his bride, the former Martha Bulloch of Rosewell, Georgia. The neighborhood was then quite fashionable. The Academy of Music, the luxurious Fifth Avenue Hotel, and the Union League Club were within easy walking distance. Horace Greeley, Peter Cooper, George Templeton Strong, and other notables lived nearby.

The future president of the United States lived at number 28 with his parents, a brother, two sisters, a grandmother, and an aunt until the autumn of 1872. The family then set off on a year-long excursion to Europe and on their return moved into a new house at 6 West Fifty-seventh Street. The principal reason for the move was that their once quiet neighborhood on Twentieth Street had been invaded by commerce. Lord and Taylor came to Broadway, half a block away, in 1869. Tiffany's, Arnold Constable, and other large establishments catering to the carriage trade followed suit, and the crowds and increased traffic proved too much for the Roosevelts to bear.

In time number 28 was taken over for commercial purposes, and by the 1890's it had been given a bow-shape cast-iron shop front. In 1916 a developer bought the house, demolished it, and erected a small commercial building on the site.

In 1919 Theodore Roosevelt died, and the Woman's Roosevelt Memorial Association came into being. After some debate the ladies who formed the association decided to commemorate the twenty-sixth president by reconstructing and furnishing the house in which he was born. In 1920 the site of number 28 was cleared and Robert Roosevelt's house, number 26, was razed to provide room for museum galleries, a reference library, and offices. The designer of the project was Theodate Pope Riddle, an eccentric architect who had the distinction of having gone down with the *Lusitania* and survived. Mrs. Riddle based the reconstruction of Theodore Roosevelt's house on photographs taken before it was demolished and on measurements of the Robert Roosevelt house made before it was torn down. Building the house and its museum-office-library wing cost $500,000 and took three years. The complex was opened to the public on October 27, 1923, the sixty-fifth anniversary of Theodore Roosevelt's birth.

Lacking photographs or contemporary descriptions of the interior and unable to find any of the family's account books, Mrs. Riddle was guided in furnishing the Birthplace by Theodore Roosevelt's two sisters, Mrs. Sheffield Cowles Sr. and Mrs. Douglas Robinson, both of whom had lived in the original house and

The construction of the open stairway in the front hall in 1923 presented a special problem, as it violated New York City's building code. A special dispensation was obtained in this instance, but otherwise the building conforms to the code. The fireproof steel-frame house has concrete floors and partitions. What appear to be molded wooden doors and doorframes are actually made of rolled steel.

Theodore Roosevelt Birthplace, 28 East Twentieth Street, New York City, 1920–1923. The main house (left) is a reconstruction designed by Theodate Pope Riddle (1868–1946) of the original 1848 building, which was demolished in 1916. The adjoining wing at the right houses offices, museum galleries, and a reference library. *Photographs are by Helga Photo Studio.*

remembered it well. Roosevelt's widow also provided helpful information, since she had frequently visited the house as a child.

The date chosen for the restoration was 1865, the year in which the elder Roosevelts hired the renowned interior decorator and cabinetmaker Léon Marcotte to refurbish what were described as fairly drab rooms. Many family recollections of the 1865 interiors were quite detailed, down to the placement of furniture, color schemes, and fabrics. Mrs. Riddle and the Woman's Roosevelt Memorial Association succeeded in recovering approximately 40 per cent of the original furnishings of the house. The balance consisted of objects that belonged to other branches of the family and period pieces with no family connection. Most of the fabrics and trimmings for draperies and upholstery, as well as wallpapers and carpets, were specially made to approximate as closely as possible those in the original house as they were recollected by former residents and visitors.

Unfortunately, little consideration was given over the years to maintaining the character of the period rooms as they were so painstakingly restored by Mrs. Riddle and the early members of the Woman's Roosevelt Memorial Association. When it came time to replace wallpapers, drapes, and upholstery, substi-

tutes were invariably selected that matched neither in pattern nor in color those used in 1923. *Objets d'art* were moved from one room to another or removed from display altogether, and the furniture was shifted about in endless combinations from year to year. To make matters worse, regular maintenance was sadly neglected even though the furniture received more than its share of nicks and scratches from visitors who were permitted to tramp through every room in the house. Additional damage was caused by the weekly receptions, award ceremonies, and teas that were held in the house from the 1920's through the 1940's.

The National Park Service acquired the house in 1963, along with Roosevelt's better-known residence, Sagamore Hill in Oyster Bay, Long Island. However, it was not until 1976 that a systematic survey was made of the Birthplace and its contents, and restoration undertaken.

Photographs of the 1923 installation were particularly helpful in duplicating the way the drapes were hung. Carpets were reproduced from small samples that had been tucked away in a closet for fifty years, and all but one of the wallpapers were matched by the Birge Wallpaper Company of Buffalo, New York, which had made them to order for the house in 1923.

The parlor was, according to Roosevelt, "a room of much splendor . . . open for general use only on Sunday evening or on rare occasions when there was a party" (*Theodore Roosevelt: An Autobiography* [New York, 1926 ed.], p. 8). The great cost of the trimmings on the curtains created a scandal in 1923: the fringe was $1.25 a yard, and the tassels cost $25 each. These have recently been replaced at more than twenty times their original cost. According to one of Roosevelt's sisters, the gas chandelier in the parlor of the original house had no globes so that each jet of gas could flicker like a candle flame. The mid-nineteenth-century marble-topped mahogany table in the view to the left and the mahogany sofas in the view below belonged to Roosevelt's grandfather Cornelius. The rosewood Gothic revival side chair was used in the 1848 house, as were the engravings above the sofas and the garniture on the mantel.

Dorothy Drahms of the company passed many hours searching Birge's archives until she discovered the document for each paper. Because Birge no longer has the facilities to print papers by hand, the company was unable to reproduce the twenty-three-color block-printed paper it had made for the parlor in 1923. The Park Service had that paper silk screened by a small firm in New York City.

The Park Service's Historic Preservation Center in Boston analyzed paint samples from every part of the house and re-established the correct colors for millwork and ceilings, based on the Munsell system. The center was also instrumental in having broken and missing hardware repaired or replaced. In addition, the prints in the house have been restored and their gilded frames repaired. Furniture has been cleaned, French-polished, and reupholstered. All the windows have been fitted with ultraviolet filters to prevent the furnishings from fading, and a complete climate-control system will soon be installed.

In short, the period rooms of the Theodore Roosevelt Birthplace once again accurately reflect the nineteenth-century interiors the young Roosevelt knew so well, and the Park Service has taken all the necessary steps to guarantee that they will remain in this condition for generations to come.

The library, or back parlor, was the family living room. Roosevelt recalled that it was filled with "chairs, tables, and bookcases of gloomy respectability" (*Autobiography*, p. 7). The Roosevelts brought back the obelisks on the mantel from a trip to Egypt in 1868. The Argand lamp on the center table is supplied (once with gas, now with electricity) from the overhead fixture, as would have been customary in the last century. The Wilton carpet here and other Wilton and Brussels carpets in the house were made to order in France for the recent restoration.

Roosevelt and his sisters complained that the horsehair upholstery of the chairs in the dining room scratched their legs. The walnut chairs now in the room were a wedding present to Roosevelt's parents-in-law, Charles and Gertrude Carow, who were married in 1853. The walnut table belonged to Roosevelt's grandfather Cornelius. The cornices here and throughout the house were molded in place in 1923. The ceiling rosettes, chimneypieces, and fireplace grates were salvaged from mid-nineteenth-century houses in the process of being demolished.

The suite of satinwood-veneer furniture with rosewood trim in the principal bedroom is original to the nineteenth-century house. According to family tradition, it was made by Léon Marcotte, who was working in New York City by 1849. When the room was restored in 1923 the original blue brocade draperies were reinstalled. Worn and faded by the late 1940's, they were discarded without a scrap being saved for the record, and were replaced by red-paisley draperies hung in the Empire manner. Blue brocade was installed again in the recent restoration. The portrait of Roosevelt's mother, Martha Bulloch Roosevelt, was painted by Jennette (or Jeanette) S. H. Loop (1840–1909) in 1874.

The nursery is almost entirely furnished with family furniture. According to family tradition, the walnut sleigh bed was made by Bernard Bosch, who worked in New York City before 1857. Above it hangs an engraving of Sir Thomas Lawrence's painting *Emily and Laura Ann Calmady* which is now in the Metropolitan Museum of Art. The tiny rush-seated chair was used by Roosevelt when he was a baby.

Old Capitol, Iowa City, Iowa

BY MARGARET N. KEYES, *Professor of home economics and director of Old Capitol, University of Iowa*

ON MAY 4, 1839, a wooden stake was driven into a bluff overlooking the Iowa River in Johnson County to mark the site of the new capitol of the Territory of Iowa. The structure standing on that spot today (Pl. I) has served as the third capitol of the Territory of Iowa,[1] the first capitol of the state of Iowa, and the first permanent home of the University of Iowa, whose campus now surrounds it. In 1839 the stake was in the midst of large groves of hickory and oak trees and extensive lime- and sandstone quarries. Indians and a few squatters were the only residents.

Chauncey Swan, one of the three commissioners charged with selecting the site, directed a survey with the stake as a starting point to develop a grid plan for the new seat of government. A draft of the first map of the city, drawn by Leander Judson, is dated July 4, 1839. It incorporated streets, alleys, market places, church sites, parks, a governor's square, and a promenade along the Iowa River.

To design the new capitol Swan enlisted John Francis Rague, a Springfield, Illinois, architect, who three years previously had submitted the winning design for the Illinois State Capitol. Rague was a native of New Jersey who had worked as a draftsman with Minard Lafever in New York in the 1820's.[2] In December 1839 Rague's plans for the Iowa capitol were accepted by the territorial legislature, and he was hired to superintend the construction of the building.[3]

The cornerstone was laid on July 4, 1840, and nine days later Rague resigned because not enough money was available to build the structure according to his design and because of the inferior quality of the stone from the nearby quarry. The exterior walls were raised under the supervision of Chauncey Swan and a succession of building supervisors. Old Capitol was first occupied on December 5, 1842, when the fifth legislative assembly of the Territory of Iowa met in rooms with unplastered walls on the first floor. The

Fig. 1. Old Capitol, Iowa City, in a photograph (possibly a daguerreotype) taken in 1853. The view is from the southeast and shows that the portico on the east side had not yet been built. However, a lithograph of the building made in the following year by George Henry Yewell (1830–1923) shows the portico in place. *University of Iowa Library, Dey collection; photograph by courtesy of the library.*

Fig. 2. Photograph of Old Capitol in 1920. This view of the west side shows the steps, platform, pediment, and recessed cornice ready for a portico which had never been built. The portico was finally added between 1921 and 1924. *Photograph by Frederick W. Kent.*

Fig. 3. Governor's office on the first floor. Heat was originally supplied by the corner fireplace, one of four so positioned on the first floor. The mantelpieces are reconstructions based on evidence found in the millwork. Sometime during the nineteenth century all these fireplaces were bricked up, and cast-iron stoves were used for heating. The stovepipe shown here leads from its original opening in the chimney to the hall, where it was connected to a stove. The oak and walnut desk in the window well would have been used by the governor's secretary, who shared his office. Over the mantel hangs an 1854 map of Iowa City. The rocking chair dates from the 1840's. *Except as noted, photographs are by Helga Photo Studio.*

Fig. 4. Corner of the Territorial-State Library on the first floor. The pine bookcases were in place in 1857 and may be original to the building. The books on their shelves are part of a collection of more than one thousand books originally in the room which were returned when the contents of the two earliest catalogues of the library were publicized by researchers working on the restoration. Each book is dated 1857 or earlier and bears the inscription *Iowa State Library* at the bottom of page 30 as required by state law. The collection includes books on law, medicine, history, travel, and other subjects since the library was intended for use by any citizen of Iowa, not just those employed in the building. Walnut armchairs of 1855–1860 are placed around a cherry drop-leaf table thought to have been made in Iowa in the 1840's. On the table are a Sandwich-glass astral lamp and a traveling desk, both of the 1850's. Against the far wall stands a coat rack of c. 1855.

second floor, where they were supposed to meet, was in an even more unfinished state. Four years later President James K. Polk signed the act that admitted Iowa to the Union, and Old Capitol, still incomplete, became the first capitol of the state.

Swan continued to be associated with the construction of the building until he left Iowa in 1849 to join the California gold rush. While William Pattee was superintendent of buildings from 1851 through 1853 the cupola was completed, and the reverse-spiral staircase (see Pl. II) and the gallery in the house of representatives chamber were installed (see Fig. 1).[4] Who designed these features remains unclear. As early as 1842 William B. Snyder, then building superintendent, reported to the Iowa legislature, "I have not been able to make an accurate estimate for the cupalo [*sic*], on account of there being no plan for the cupalo (nor for anything else) in the Superintendent's office when I received it. . . ."[5] Rague himself wrote in 1856, "I made the plans for the Iowa Capitol although I do not speak of the latter building with any degree of pride in as much as the plans were not carried out."[6] However, given the strong similarity of the Illinois and Iowa capitols, he surely meant that his plans had not been carried out as he had intended.[7]

As early as 1847 the Iowa legislature passed a law which stated that Old Capitol would be given to the newly established University of Iowa when a site for a new capital farther to the west had been located. In 1857 Des Moines was made the state capital, and the university received Old Capitol as its first permanent structure. Even then the building was not finished, and the legislators appropriated money for its completion after moving to Des Moines.

Despite these funds the west portico was not built until a major remodeling of the building was undertaken between 1921 and 1924. A photograph taken in 1920 shows that Rague's intention was to build a portico on the west side to balance the east one (Fig. 2).

Beginning in 1857 the university used Old Capitol for offices, classrooms, a library, and a chapel where compulsory daily services were held. At one point during the nineteenth century, the Iowa City fire department was housed there, and during the Civil War it was used by both the city and the university as an armory. Other university departments that have had

Pl. I. Old Capitol in Iowa City, designed by John Francis Rague (1799–1877), built 1840–1857, remodeled 1921–1924, and restored 1970–1976. The building is now a National Historic Landmark, and the four-block area around it is listed on the National Register of Historic Places as a National Historic District.

Pl. II. Reverse-spiral staircase leading from the first to the second floor. It was installed during the 1921–1924 remodeling and is nearly identical to the original stair.

quarters there include nineteenth-century literary societies, archives, the alumni association, and, most recently, the central administration of the university.

Nineteenth-century photographs attest to the fact that, except for the addition of the west portico, the exterior of Old Capitol has remained unchanged since 1857. What Talbot Hamlin has called "a simple but excellently designed building,"[8] Old Capitol is 120 feet long, 60 feet wide, and 60 feet from ground level to ridge pole. The cupola with its base is 54 feet tall. The building is of limestone, the steps are granite, and the Doric porticoes are largely of wood painted to resemble stone.

Despite many changes, the basic integrity of the interior has been maintained, particularly the central rotunda, the spiral staircase from the first to the second floor, and the millwork throughout.

In 1970 the president of the university, Willard L. Boyd, announced that Old Capitol was to be restored. A committee of volunteers was formed, with Mrs. Virgil M. Hancher, the widow of a long-time university president, as its chairman. The committee decided to restore the building to represent its three periods of occupancy—territorial (1842–1846), state (1846–1857), and university (1857–1970)—and to use it as a meeting place for appropriate state, academic, historical, and cultural functions, in addition to opening it to the public. The Springfield, Illinois, architectural firm of Ferry and Henderson was hired as consultants.

During the 1920's remodeling, Old Capitol had been fireproofed according to the standards of the time and many interior changes had been made. Research was undertaken to determine the arrangement and appearance of the rooms between 1842 and 1857, the territorial and state years. Rague's floor plans were not located, but an 1840 committee described the intended appearance of both the exterior and the interior:

. . . the basement story is entered by two doors in the opposite ends, both opening into a hall seven feet wide, which runs directly through the building north and south, dividing it into two equal parts. There are four rooms on each side about twenty feet square, designed for committee rooms. There is also a large and convenient wood-room and a fire-proof vault, arched with brick, and covered with grouted masonry, more than three feet thick, for the safety of public documents. On the next floor there is the same division north and south, and a broad hall or vestibule east and west, entered from the porticos on each side of the building. North of the vestibule, east side, is a room forty-three by twenty-two and a half feet, designed for the supreme court; a corresponding room of the same size on the south of the vestibule, is designed for the use of the Secretary of the Territory. West of the north and south hall are four rooms, equal in size, designed for the use of the Governor, Auditor, Treasurer, and the Library. On the upper floor the north and south hall is omitted. In the south wing is the Representatives hall, fifty-two by forty-three feet in the clear. In the north wing are the Council chamber and three small committee rooms, cut off from the west of it.[9]

In 1970 the rooms on the second floor were as indicated in the report except for the three committee rooms, which had never been constructed, but many changes had been made in the plan of the first floor. The supreme court chamber had been divided into three offices, and the secretary of the territory's office had been made into two rooms: the university president's office and an adjoining reception room. The four rooms of equal size on the west side of the floor had been completely changed; those on the north side of the central hall had been made into one large room, and those on the south side had been divided into three offices.

Removal of all the interior plaster showed that the four rooms of equal size on the first floor had been built as originally planned, but no evidence of the walls of the three second-floor committee rooms was found.

With two exceptions, all the rooms have been made their original size and furnished to represent the years 1842 to 1857. The exceptions are the president's office (Fig. 6) with its adjacent reception room and the senate chamber (Fig. 5). Both have been made to look as much as possible as they did after the remodeling of the 1920's, with furnishings that represent the university's period of occupancy of Old Capitol.

The present staircase from the first to the second floor was installed during the 1920's remodeling, and although it is patterned after the original, it varies in several details (Pl. II). One of the newel posts of the original staircase was ten inches higher than the other, probably because the builders could not cope with the fast descent of the inside rail and the gradual descent of the outside one. The newel posts are now both of equal height. In the 1920's remodeling, the shape of the second-floor landing was altered and the ribbed underside of the staircase was made smooth. Also in that remodeling, a spiral staircase from the first floor to the ground floor replaced the original straight staircase. That stair also remains in place today.

Furnishing the rooms of the 1842–1857 period required extensive research. There is evidence that the furniture used in the first territorial capitol at Burlington from 1838 to 1842 was brought in wagons to Iowa City in the latter year. Then, when Des Moines was made the state capital in 1857, the furnishings of Old Capitol were taken there during the winter. According to surviving accounts, some of the oxcarts and bobsleds used for the 1857 move bogged down in snow and mud and were left to rot. Whether any of the original furnishings reached Des Moines is not known, but none are in the present state capitol there.

Fig. 6. President's office on the first floor. The walnut paneling and millwork date from the 1920's renovation of the office, which was used by fifteen of the sixteen presidents of the university from 1860 until 1970. The desk and the chair drawn up to it were also used by various presidents of the university.

The decision was made to continue searching for objects originally in Old Capitol but if none were found to seek nineteenth-century furnishings appropriate for use in a legislative building in frontier Iowa. Other capitols of the period were studied, including the Illinois capitol in Springfield and the North Carolina capitol in Raleigh.

Clues in the form of bills of sale, vouchers, and receipts were sought in many historical repositories in Iowa and were finally located in the National Archives in Washington, D.C. Most items were listed only in general terms, but at least evidence was available that desks, chairs, secretaries, benches, quill pens, spittoons, ink, black sand, and many other furnishings had been purchased.

One particularly helpful voucher of 1839 included "Twenty-six cane chairs."[10] Because there were twenty-six members in the house of representatives in 1839, when the capital was Burlington, it was assumed that the chairs were for the members of the house. Presumably, these chairs were then transferred to the capitol in Iowa City in 1842.

In July 1974 a major discovery was made. An advertisement for an auction in What Cheer, Iowa, in-

Pl. III. House of representatives chamber on the second floor. For years this and the senate chamber (Fig. 5) were identical in appearance. However, when the walls were stripped of plaster in 1972 evidence was found of the visitors' gallery frequently referred to in written records. The gallery, probably removed sometime in the last century, has been reconstructed. The desks and chairs are reproductions of those originally in this room (see Pl. VIII, Fig. 8). The reproduction Brussels carpet is patterned on a mid-nineteenth-century prototype. The speaker's podium is modeled on podiums of the 1840's and 1850's in other state capitols and incorporates some elements of the design of the house chamber. The twenty-nine-star American flag commemorates Iowa's admission to the Union as the twenty-ninth state in 1846. The brass candlesticks and ceramic spittoons all date from the nineteenth century.

cluded a "walnut armchair (from the Old State Capitol in Iowa City)." The design and construction of the chair seemed appropriate for the years 1842 to 1857, and stamped under the seat was the inscription *State of Iowa, Custodians*. The seat and back had originally been caned, but by 1974 the chair was upholstered (see Pl. VIII). The armchair was assumed to be one of those originally in the house chamber, and eight others have since been located because of publicity about the first one.

Two of the original desks from the house chamber were found after an extensive search, the first one in Florida and the second at Grinnell College in Grinnell, Iowa (see Fig. 8). The wedge-shape tops of the two desks gave a valuable clue to their arrangement in a semicircle in the chamber. Walnut reproductions of the original chairs and desks were made by the Norman Schanz Company in Iowa's Amana Colony in West Amana, since it was not thought possible that all twenty-six original chairs and desks would be found.

Records of the textiles purchased for the capitol were also fragmentary and imprecise. The carpet on the floor of the house chamber is a reproduction of a Brussels carpet of 1840–1850 which includes Greek revival motifs that complement elements of Old Capitol. Other rugs used in the restoration are examples of nineteenth-century ingrain carpets and hand-woven rag rugs. Curtains have not been planned for the building because replicas of the original paneled wood interior shutters have been installed at all windows and are used to control the light.

Heating, air-conditioning, and humidity-control systems have been concealed in baseboards and cornices, but the mid-nineteenth-century appearance of the rooms has been preserved by the restoration of the four original fireplaces on the first floor and the use of reproduction cast-iron stoves on both the first and second floors. Stovepipes have been placed in holes in

Pl. IV. Supreme court chamber on the first floor. The modern judges' bench is based on comparable benches in other state capitols of the mid-nineteenth century. The windsor benches and chairs and the walnut tables date from the 1840's. Lighting fixtures include two tole whale-oil chandeliers, c. 1830, and two astral lamps marked by Cornelius and Company of Philadelphia, 1845–1853.

Fig. 7. Desk - and - bookcase. Scott County, Iowa, 1840. Black walnut with walnut burl; height 91¼, width 42⅛, depth (of bottom) 20⅝ inches. The desk-and-bookcase is now in the Territorial-State Library.

Fig. 8. Desk from the house of representatives chamber, possibly by Evan Evans (1806–1892), Burlington, Iowa, c. 1839. Black walnut and pine; height 29, width (of front) 35¼, depth 23¾ inches. The top is covered with oilcloth as was typical of the 1830's. This is one of two models from which the replicas in the restored house chamber were made. It may be the work of Evan Evans, a Burlington cabinetmaker, since an 1839 voucher indicates that he was paid for making desks for the territorial legislative assembly in Burlington. *On permanent loan from Grinnell College, Grinnell, Iowa.*

the chimneys which were discovered bricked up when the plaster was stripped.

Nineteenth-century furnishings have been selected for their appropriateness to a government building. They include Bennington spittoons; brass candlesticks with handmade tallow candles; tole whale-oil chandeliers; camphene, whale-oil, astral, and sinumbra lamps; cast-iron andirons; ceramic ink bottles; and wood sand shakers. All books in the chambers and offices are Iowa government and legal books of the period. The Territorial-State Library (Pl. VII, Fig. 4) contains a collection of more than one thousand books which were originally in that room.[11] Many are shelved in a bank of five bookcases which were in use in Old Capitol as early as 1857 and may possibly be original to the building. Some objects are reproductions, among them the handmade quill pens in polished pewter holders, which are the work of Lewis Glaser, a Charlottesville, Virginia, craftsman.

In the future, twenty-seven electrified ormolu sconces with frosted-glass globes will be installed on the walls of the first- and second-floor halls, and more floor coverings and other textiles will be added to the furnishings of the building.

Old Capitol, the first public building in Iowa to undergo a major restoration, was reopened to the public on July 3, 1976. At that time it was designated a National Historic Landmark.

Fig. 9. Second-floor hall. The Corinthian columns are of pine and the capitals are identical to Minard Lafever's drawing of a capital "from the Monument of Lysicrates" *(The Beauties of Modern Architecture* [New York, 1835], Pl. 43). Since Rague worked for Lafever, these columns may have been a part of his original design for the capitol.

[1] From 1838 until sometime in 1842 the legislators met in the first territorial capitol in Burlington, Iowa. The fourth legislative assembly of the Territory of Iowa met in a temporary capitol in Iowa City in 1842.

[2] Betsy H. Woodman, "John Francis Rague: Mid-Nineteenth Century Revivalist Architect" (master's thesis, University of Iowa, 1969), p. 6.

[3] *Journal of the House of Representatives of the Second Legislative Assembly of the Territory of Iowa* (Burlington, Iowa, 1840), p. 94. The contract had actually been signed on November 12, 1839, according to a notice in the *Iowa Territorial Gazette*, Burlington.

[4] *Acts, Resolutions and Memorials Passed at the Regular Session of the Fourth General Assembly of the State of Iowa* [1852] (Iowa City, 1853), p. 142.

[5] *Journal of the Council of the Fifth Legislative Assembly of the Territory of Iowa* [1842] (Davenport, Iowa, 1843), p. 216.

[6] John F. Rague to P. M. Casady, Dubuque, May 15, 1856; Phineas M. Casady collection, no. C261, manuscript division, Iowa State Historical Department, division of Historical and Museum and Archives, Des Moines.

[7] Henry-Russell Hitchcock and William Seale compare the Iowa and Illinois capitols, noting their unmistakable similarities and their differences and crediting the latter to the layman (or laymen) who continued Rague's work after he left the project *(Temples of Democracy: The State Capitols of the U.S.A.* [New York and London, 1976], pp. 108–110).

[8] *Greek Revival Architecture in America* (London and New York, 1944), p. 255.

[9] *Journal of the House of Representatives of the Third Legislative Assembly of the Territory of Iowa* [1840] (Dubuque, 1841), pp. 191–192.

[10] Legislative and Contingent Expenses of the Territory of Iowa, 1839, account no. 80, 345, National Archives, Washington, D.C.

[11] These books are recorded in the first two catalogues made of the library's holdings. The "Catalogue of Territorial Library Made by Librarian [Theodore S.] Parvin in 1839" was published in Johnson Brigham, "Pioneer History of the Territorial and State Library of Iowa, II," *Annals of Iowa* (3rd series), vol. 10, no. 8 (January 1913), pp. 590–628. The second catalogue is *Catalogue of the Iowa Territorial Library*, compiled by Morgan Reno (Iowa City, 1845).

Pl. V. Treasurer's office on the first floor. The iron safe, walnut desks and pigeonholes, table, camphene lamp on the table, and coat rack all date from the mid-nineteenth century. Over the safe hangs an 1839 map of the Territory of Iowa.

Pl. VI. Office of the auditor on the first floor. The walnut stand-up desk was made in Iowa c. 1845. All the documents in the pigeonholes are copies of originals of the 1840's and 1850's. On the floor is a nineteenth-century ingrain carpet, one of several used in the building.

Pl. VII. Territorial-State Library (see also Fig. 4). The walnut side chairs and drop-leaf table date from c. 1845, the Sandwich glass astral lamp, c. 1850.

Pl. VIII. Governor's office on the first floor (see also Fig. 3). The large walnut desk was made in Iowa in the 1840's. On it are a sinumbra lamp of 1825 and a rosewood and walnut traveling desk of c. 1840. The walnut chair on the far side of the desk is one of the few original pieces of furniture from the capitol that have been located to date. Originally caned, it is from the house of representatives chamber and served as the model for the reproductions now in the chamber. The walnut desk-and-bookcase is a mid-nineteenth-century Iowa piece. The pedestal table in front of the window is pine, c. 1830. The Philadelphia windsor chair of 1800–1810 beside it was brought to Iowa by a Virginia family on its way west. On the floor is a mid-nineteenth-century ingrain carpet.

The Sam Davis Home, Smyrna, Tennessee

BY ELISABETH DONAGHY GARRETT

Pulaski, Giles County, Tenn., Nov. 26, 1863
Dear Mother, Oh how painful it is to write to you. I have got to die tomorrow morning—to be hung by the federals. Mother do not grieve for me. I must bid you goodbye forever more—Mother I do not hate to die. Give my love to all. Your Dear Son, Sam.

Mother tell the children, all to be good, I wish I could see all of you once more, but I never never no more.

Mother and Father, do not forget me, think of me when I am dead, but do not grieve for me, it will not do any good.

Father, You can send after my remains if you want to do so, they will be at Pulaski Tenn. I will leave some things too with the hotel keeper for you.

Pulaski is in Giles Co. Tenn., South of Columbia.[1]

ON THE MORNING of the following day, November 27, 1863, the youthful soldier and Confederate scout Sam Davis was hanged as a spy by order of General Grenville M. Dodge of the Union army. The twenty-one-year-old hero of the Confederacy denied the spying charge until the end and refused a promise of freedom in return for divulging the source of the incriminating papers found on him. Asked at the foot of the scaffold if it would not have been better to have accepted the offer of life, the tenacious Tennessee youth replied, "Do you suppose that I would betray a friend? No, sir; I would die a thousand times first!"[2]

Sam Davis Home, its outbuildings, and some of the large, handsome oak trees which still enhance the property. The photograph dates from c. 1905. *Photograph by courtesy of the Sam Davis Home.*

Sam Davis Home. When Charles Davis moved into the house in 1847 he covered a log cabin of c. 1810 with poplar siding and built the portico at its center. At the same time he added the rear, or north, wing with what is now called the family room, a dining room, and bedrooms. The spacious house has eight rooms with two stairways leading to separate sections of the second floor. *Except as noted, photographs are by Helga Photo Studio.*

Section of the L-shape porch which parallels both the main house and the rear wing. A towel hangs above a bucket of water and a ladle on the table. "This is very much according to the custom here," wrote a Scottish traveler to the South in 1830. "The water is brought in a large pewter bason, and is set down . . . where there is a large towel upon a roller" (James Stuart, *Three Years in North America*, Edinburgh, 1833, vol. 2, p. 189). In the background, beyond the boxwood, is an Italian marble shaft which seventeen members of the Coleman Scout Patrol erected in 1866 in memory of their companion. It is inscribed, "A truer soldier, a purer patriot, a braver man, never lived. He suffered death on the gibbet rather than betray his friend and country."

The charge and the sentence were too severe for the scout, who should have been treated as an ordinary prisoner of war. But this was only one of the many injustices committed in the name of that fratricidal horror, the Civil War. Even Union soldiers who witnessed the execution praised Sam Davis' heroism, but his memory has been particularly dear to his fellow Tennesseans who lost so much and suffered so greatly in the war. The tale of Sam Davis is a familiar one in literature, but it is perhaps in his boyhood home in Smyrna, Tennessee, that his memory is most vividly kept alive. It was to there that his pathetic letter of November 26 was sent, and there that he is buried.

The 168-acre Davis farm is what remains today of some seven hundred acres which comprised the family plantation before the Civil War.[3] Charles Lewis Davis and his wife, Jane Simmons, moved to the farm in 1847. With its house on a rise overlooking green fields and Stewart's Creek, the farm is a microcosm of central Tennessee's fertile acres laced with streams. No wonder Sam confessed to one Union soldier that "life was sweet and he would like to live to see the end of it."[4]

Front parlor. The window cornice and lambrequin are original to the room, as are the four Victorian side chairs, the sofa (one of a pair), an easy chair (not visible), and the Brussels carpet. An 1875 inventory of the estate of Charles L. Davis lists "Parlor Furniture, ½ Doz. chairs, 2 easy chairs, 2 Divans, 1 Centre Table, 1 Piano Fort, 1 Brussels Carpet." The cherry candle-stand was made locally. The fireplace is one of eight, all of which have wooden surrounds. The wallpaper is a reproduction of a paper of c. 1850 found in a house in Murfreesboro, Tennessee. The border in this room and the other wallpapers in the house are also reproductions of nineteenth-century papers.

Back parlor. The portrait of Sam Davis over the mantel is hypothetical and posthumous, as there are no known pictures of him during his lifetime. The Brussels or Wilton carpet is woven in tones of red and yellow. Flanking the fireplace are a secretary and a chest of drawers, both of walnut and tulipwood. An eight-day clock by E. C. Brewster and Company of Bristol, Connecticut, is on the chest.

Hall between the two parlors. The stairway retains its original cherry balustrade and handrail and leads to the bedroom which Sam shared with his brother Oscar.

The handsome clapboard house is important not only as the childhood home of a Confederate hero but as a well-preserved and well-maintained example of an antebellum, upper-middle-class farmhouse in Middle Tennessee. Wilma Dykeman in her poetic portrait of Tennessee has written, "Tennesseans have believed in the gun, the Bible, and themselves—not necessarily in that order, but all together."[5] The Sam Davis Home with its strong, land-loving, God-fearing family scarred by violence seems to embody this description.

Sam's younger brother Oscar lived in the house until his death in 1927. Oscar's son sold the farm to the state of Tennessee on December 20, 1927. The property was deeded in trust to the Sam Davis Memorial Association which pledged "to beautify, preserve, and adorn" the property and "to acquire, own and display all historic or literary productions, relics, mementoes relating to, and otherwise memorializing his life and character. . . ."[6] The association immediately began acquiring some of the original furnishings and other appropriate pieces of the period. Today, with its sturdy locally made furniture of walnut and cherry, its strip and ingrain carpeting, and its colorful wallpapers, the house is indeed a worthy tribute to the family who raised such an honorable and independent young Tennessean.

Simple rural furniture and an ingrain carpet in Sam's bedroom suggest a farm family of comfortable means. The rocker, with its handsome turnings, and the side chairs were made locally. Decoration on the walnut and tulipwood desk is restricted to the serpentine-crestings of the pigeonholes. The bold, solidly built walnut cupboard with its emphatic dentils was probably made in the vicinity. The eight-day mantel clock is marked GRAHAM & CO. BRISTOL and was made c. 1864. Sam's grandmother made the quilt on the bed around 1836. Charles Lewis' 1875 estate inventory listed "8 Bed Steads & Bedding."

[1] Quoted in Owen Nichols Meredith, *The Sam Davis Home*, reprinted from the *Tennessee Historical Quarterly* (winter 1965), pp. 13-14.

[2] *Ibid.*, p. 15.

[3] *Ibid.*, p. 3.

[4] *Ibid.*, p. 8.

[5] Wilma Dykeman, *Tennessee: A Bicentennial History* (New York, 1975), p. 17.

[6] Meredith, *Sam Davis Home*, p. 18.

The strip carpeting in the dining room is original and the curtains are copies of the originals. The wallpaper is a reproduction of a paper in the James Gallier House in New Orleans. The portrait over the mantel depicts Mrs. Henry (Lucy Searcy) White, a friend of Mrs. Davis. The 1860 Audubon print depicts eider ducks. The dining-room table, chairs, side table, and sugar chest are all of cherry. The table is set with Davis family dessert plates and silverware by various American silversmiths.

Both the chair and the yarn winder in the foreground of the "girls' room" were made locally; the rag rugs were braided by nieces of Sam Davis to replace worn originals. The 1860's sewing machine under the window was owned by the Davis family.

Strip carpeting covers the floor of the family room. The rocking chairs were used by Mrs. Charles Davis, as were the brown gingham bonnet and cashmere shawl on the smaller rocker, which retains traces of its original blue-green paint. The mantel clock was made and sold by Chauncey Jerome in Bristol, Connecticut, where he worked from 1822 to 1844. The brasses that still remain on the walnut chest of drawers are original. It has quarter columns at the front corners and tall bracket feet. Sam's monkey doll sits in the Davis family cherry cradle. The simple washstand suggest the five washstands mentioned in the 1875 inventory.

The desk in the foreground of this view of the family room supports a Davis family ledger of 1865.

The smokehouse is one of three extant outbuildings. There were originally some twenty structures on the estate, but today only the smokehouse, kitchen, and overseer's office remain. Some log slave cabins have been rebuilt on their original sites. An 1860 census indicates that there were fourteen slave cabins on the Charles Davis estate.

The kitchen is in a separate building. An assortment of locally made furniture and produce suggests the sort of scene that would have lured Sam and his brothers and sisters to the door.

Old Richmond, the Houston guest cottage of Mr. and Mrs. Fred T. Couper Jr.

BY ELISABETH DONAGHY GARRETT

IN AMIABLE and serene surroundings of green lawns and brilliant azaleas, empyreal pines, and august oaks, a venerable survivor of pioneer times in Texas is enjoying a peaceful and prosperous old age. The survivor is Old Richmond, the guest cottage of Mr. and Mrs. Fred T. Couper Jr. of Houston.

With its Greek revival symmetry of plan and columned porch, Old Richmond is an accurate rendition of the early

Pl. I. Old Richmond was built to counteract the oppressive heat of the long Texas summer and to take advantage of the prevailing southerly breeze from the Gulf of Mexico. It is raised on brick piers, allowing for circulation of air underneath it, and has both front and side porches (see Pl. XIV). There are twenty large windows, including the floor-length (nine and one-half feet tall) windows across the façade, which can be raised the full height of the lower sash. The unusual number and size of the windows, most with their original glass, provide for light and cheerful rooms. For warmth there are three original fireplaces. Air conditioning and central heating are modern conveniences added by the Coupers at the time of restoration. *Photographs are by Helga Photo Studio.*

Texas frame house. Fortuitous Victorian additions were the delightful jig-sawn brackets and porch balustrade and the tin decoration on the roof that extends the length of the ridgepole and shows a Texas star and clover leaf.

Old Richmond was built about 1850 in Richmond, Texas, then a town of some two hundred citizens, in the big bend of the river Brazos de Dios (Arms of God). Situated a block from the courthouse, the house was lived in by a succession of prominent Richmond citizens. When it was threatened with demolition in 1974 to make way for a large bank building, Old Richmond was given to Mary Frances Bowles Couper by her cousins Dr. and Mrs. Joe C. Wessendorff. Dr. Wessendorff is the grandson of Dr. J. C. Johnson, a Richmond surgeon whose family had lived in the house for many years at the turn of the twentieth century. Mrs. Couper made plans to move the cottage to the grounds of her Houston house, Piney Point, thirty miles northeast of Richmond. Both the Richmond and the Houston sites were among the three hundred original Texas land grants which the enlightened

Pl. II. The thirty-seven-foot-long entrance hall opens onto the front and side porches, providing coolness and light. The pine floors, deep baseboards, and simple moldings are original throughout. The wallpapers are modern adaptations of earlier designs. Spring bouquets of forsythia and mock orange overflow a pair of mahogany and brass plant stands of about 1835. The deep-green painted Baltimore settee and a pair of Baltimore fancy chairs also in the hall were received with a history of original ownership in a Greek revival house in Alloway, New Jersey. An oil portrait of the American clipper ship *Adelaide* hangs above the settee. The *Adelaide* was also pictured off Sandy Hook around 1856 as the first illustration in Currier and Ives' Sail series. Opening off the hall to the right are double parlors with sliding doors. Two bedrooms of comparable size open off the hall to the left.

Pl. III. Rich wallpaper adds intensity to an already cheerfully bright front parlor. On the mantel of one of the original fireplaces is a pair of bronze and ormolu candleholders. Made in France around 1835, they have frosted-glass shades painted with garlands of fruit. Handsome New York open-arm chairs of around 1825 flank the fireplace. They are mahogany with secondary woods of pine, poplar, and beech. The swivel-top mahogany card table is a particularly fine example of the Boston Empire style. There are cut-brass inlays of anthemia on the skirt and base and ormolu rosettes at the corners of the skirt. The leaf-carved pedestal flows into a spiral twist at the top. The hurricane shade on the table is one of a pair of very large early nineteenth-century shades etched with flower-filled urns. Each square of the colorful needlework rug of about 1840, with its bouquets of various flowers, was signed by the lady who stitched it. The chandelier was made in France in the late nineteenth century.

Pl. IV. Another view of the front parlor. The Empire sofa with its striking veneers, dolphin arms, and carved paw feet with winged cornucopia was probably made in Philadelphia around 1820. The pair of Boston side chairs with leaf-carved stay rails dates from the same period. The delicate lyre-base table is English. A pair of Empire wall sconces retaining their original shades flanks a painting entitled *The Garden Gate,* by Thomas Hicks (1823-1890), a first cousin of Edward Hicks.

Stephen F. Austin had settled by 1825. Old Richmond's new home was described in the original Mexican grant as being on Arroyo Cibolo (Buffalo Bayou) at the place "llamado Punto Pino" (called Piney Point).

Six months were spent dismantling the house, which was in good structural condition, for the move to Houston. Later additions of three rooms, a bay window, and hardwood floors (over the original pine boards) were removed.

Old Richmond arrived at Piney Point at four o'clock one misty morning. Windowless, roofless, boarded up, divided into two sections, and leaning perilously, this specter was a bewildering and disheartening sight for its new owners. Today, fully restored and handsomely furnished with nineteenth-century American antiques and some early English family pieces, this charming and venerable pioneer instills a feeling of warmth and happiness and brings a smile of pleasure to those fortunate enough to pass time within its walls.

Pl. V. This stunning example of Philadelphia Empire craftsmanship of around 1820 almost seems to have been made for this space between the two front windows of the front parlor. The fine detailing of the secretary suggests the handiwork of Anthony G. Quervelle (1789-1856). The blue-and-apricot porcelain is part of a *vieux Paris* tea service.

Pl. VI. Bouquets of yellow roses and mock orange appropriately arranged in Victorian vases exemplify the detailed charm of Old Richmond. The floral needlework rug in this back parlor or music room was made around 1840. Musical trophies and the name *Riley Thurston* are painted on the nameboard of the New York piano of around 1825. Brass roundels stamped with designs of bees and beehives surmount the six pineapple-and-spiral-twist legs. The New York fancy chair and the one visible in the hall are two of a set of six now in the cottage that date from around 1830. The Philadelphia card table with its octagonal top and leaf-carved pedestal is one of a pair. *Vieux Paris* dessert plates flank an American Argand lamp of around 1845. The girandole mirror was probably made in England in the early nineteenth century.

51

Pl. VII. An English cross-stitch rug of around 1850 brightens the floor of the library. The pineapple-carved posts of what is probably a rural New England secretary echo the luxuriant harvest of pineapples on the wallpaper. Staffordshire figures, animals, castles, and cottages are displayed inside the secretary, which has unusual stamped brass mounts. The leaf-carved pedestal of the card table and the carved tablets at the rounded corners of the skirt denote Philadelphia craftsmanship. The finely-detailed shelf clock was made by Mark Leavenworth (1774-1849) of Waterbury, Connecticut. The hands are pierced in the design of an eagle and shield.

Pl. VIII. The early nineteenth-century Chinese rug, tulip-pattern wallpaper, and *vieux Paris* dessert service in the dining room are all characterized by shades of blue and floral motifs. The late eighteenth-century mahogany dining table and chairs are English and belonged to Mrs. Couper's parents. Early nineteenth-century card tables from Salem, Massachusetts, flank the fireplace. A pair of English crystal and gilt-bronze candelabra on the mantel helps illuminate the twilight landscape by Asher B. Durand (1796-1886).

Pl. IX. The looking glass, with its painted land-scape panel, was made in New England.

Pl. X. Flowers are again the theme in the front bedroom, where the floral arabesques of the English needlepoint rug are reiterated in the finely embroidered *mousseline* bedspread and the prim bouquets of the wallpaper of Victorian inspiration. A New England looking glass hangs above a bow-front chest which is a family piece. The Gothic revival side chair, one of four in the bedroom, was made in New York around 1840.

Pl. XI. The *mousseline* bedspread and side hangings were made in France around 1850 and now complement a mid-nineteenth-century walnut bed from Texas or Louisiana.

Pl. XII. The winsome personality of Old Richmond is evident in the back bedroom (Pl. XIII) and its adjoining powder room. The mahogany marble-topped washstand is fitted with a basin that has been painted with flowers to match the wallpaper.

Pl. XIII. The Victorian bedroom furniture was Mrs. Couper's as a child and the pink bedspread with its scattering of light-blue bowknots recalls one she was fond of in her girlhood. The bed drapery is suspended from an English Victorian crown of *doré*.

Pl. XIV. The white picket garden fence seen in this side view of Old Richmond was moved with the cottage from its original location. The library and dining room are housed in the rear wing. The dining room opens to the side porch, which has been glassed in.

Pl. XV. A tiny guest kitchen has been installed at the end of the porch. The kitchen wallpaper is an anthology of birds, many of which are frequent visitors to Old Richmond and its encircling azaleas, pines, and oaks.

The restoration of
San Francisco (St. Frusquin), Reserve, Louisiana

BY HENRY W. KROTZER JR.

IN 1973 THE Energy Corporation of Louisiana, Limited (ECOL) purchased San Francisco (once called St. Frusquin) plantation in Reserve, Louisiana, as the site for an oil refinery. At the instigation and insistence of Frederick B. Ingram, a New Orleans businessman and philanthropist, the decision was made to preserve the plantation house (Pl. I), a conspicuous Victorian building on the east bank of the Mississippi River about an hour's drive upriver from New Orleans. Late in the year the architectural firm of Koch and Wilson, of which I am a partner, was retained to handle the restoration of the house. In 1974 the National Park Service declared the house a National Historic Landmark, and by late 1975 the ownership of the house and site had been turned over to a private foundation funded by ECOL and associated companies. In the autumn of 1976 Marathon Oil Company purchased the refinery from ECOL, and has continued funding the restoration through the foundation.

Early in 1974 we prepared schematic plans of the house and site, worked out preliminary construction budgets, and began to collect photographs and to do archival research.

The parish records at Edgard revealed that the plantation had been assembled from smaller properties by a free man of color, Elisée Rilliéux,[1] and sold in 1830 to Edmond Bozonier Marmillion (1803-1856) and a partner. In 1843 E. B. Marmillion's wife died, leaving him with three sons, Pierre Edmond (1826-1852), Antoine Valsin (1827-1871), and Charles (1840-1875). According to one tradition the house was built in 1849 by Antoine Valsin Marmillion. However, he would only have been twenty-two years old

in that year, and in the following year the United States census shows that he was not living at the plantation. Nowhere have we found contemporary descriptions of the house or records relating to its construction,[2] but we were able to identify the builder of the house from a clue we found during restoration. When we removed a window apron board and laid it face down on the floor, the archaeologists noticed the initials *E B M*, for Edmond Bozonier Marmillion, painted across the back. We found the same initials on the back of much of the millwork in the house, and we surmise that they were applied at the factory to identify the order.

We have dated the building of the house to between 1853 and 1856 because our research showed that there was a major break in the levee in 1852 and a bumper sugar-cane crop in 1853-1854. The first event could well have destroyed or severely damaged the house then inhabited by the Marmillions, while the subsequent profitable crop could have provided the money to build the present house.

When E. B. Marmillion died in 1856 Antoine Valsin, probably by then married to Louise de Seybold, took over the management of the plantation, which was then called simply by the owner's name. In 1859 it was renamed St. Frusquin (a play on *sans fruscins*, "without a cent") and in 1879 it was renamed again, this time San Francisco. In 1870 Antoine Valsin and Charles, a bachelor, bought out the interest of Pierre Edmond's heirs. After the deaths of Antoine Valsin and Charles, the plantation descended to Antoine Valsin's widow, Louise de Seybold Marmillion,[3] and her three daughters. They sold it in 1879 to Achille D. Bougère[4]—furnished, according to oral tradition. The Bougères say they took the contents of the house with them when they sold the house to the Ory family in 1905. Most of the furniture is said to have burned in

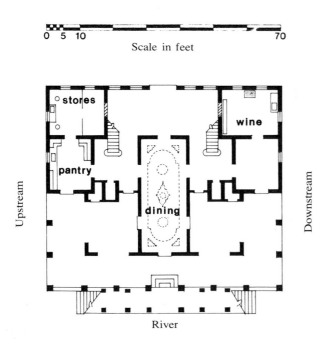

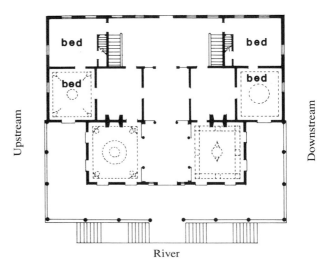

Fig. 1.   Ground-floor plan of San Francisco. *Scale drawing by Koch and Wilson, Architects.*

Fig. 2.   Main-, or second-floor plan of San Francisco. *Scale drawing by Koch and Wilson, Architects.*

level, and later one of the stairs had been removed entirely. On two sides of the main-floor entry hall the doors and their flanking fixed panels had been removed (see Fig. 7).

From the beginning we had to decide on a method of protecting the building from fire even though it was decided not to have facilities in the house such as toilets or a serving kitchen for receptions. Another early consideration was climate control. Briefly, here is what we did in these areas, based upon meetings of the restoration team at which each member discussed his requirements.

A Halon-gas fire-extinguishing system was designed. It would have offered a very effective means of stopping a fire with minimum damage to the contents except in the attic, which is entirely banded at floor level with louvers, making the room a ventilator. (It was obviously never the ballroom it was credited to be in one local tradition.) To trap Halon in this great space, automatically descending steel screens were designed to seal off the louvers should a fire start. But the complexity of the system was unsettling, and eventually we decided to recommend the familiar and simpler system of water sprinklers, accepting the fact that some pipes of the sprinkler system and most of the fire-detecting devices would be visible. Had the house contained the original furnishings, we would probably have used the Halon system regardless of its complexity.

Climate control, too, was analyzed from various points of view. A good flow of air and a certain amount of heat in winter would preserve the house and contents. However, given the extreme heat and dampness of Louisiana, we felt that a normal modern heating and air-conditioning system that provided a comfortable, low-humidity interior

climate might well cause excessive expansion and contraction of the wood that would be especially damaging to the painted wood ceilings. We finally decided that the primary requirement was to protect the interior from outside dirt and dust and that we needed a central heating and air-conditioning system that would closely follow the exterior temperature and maintain relatively high humidity. Thus, if the system were to fail, the damp exterior air entering the building would not cause the woodwork to swell unduly. The air-distributing units for the ground floor were put inside the original closets which were built against the base of the chimneys; those for the main floor were easily housed in the attic and send air through grilles in the ceiling or slits in the cornices.

Actual work on the house started with the archaeologists' analysis of its fabric. For years two visible painted ceilings had been greatly admired. On two other wooden ceilings, later overpainting had peeled off, revealing areas of penciled designs which had long been considered fragmentary cartoons for uncompleted decorations. On an early visit to the house with the archaeologists we examined the ceiling of the downstream front parlor in a strong raking light and the impasto revealed a complete design, not a fragmentary cartoon. The same thing was found to be true of the other peeling ceiling. At first we thought that the fifth painted ceiling in the house, that in the dining room, had been overpainted. Later we found it had simply been covered with a homemade organic compound that came away quite readily.

The contract with the archaeologists was expanded to include laboratory tests to see if the overpainting could be removed, which was doubtful, and to record the original work so that the painting could be reproduced later.

Pl. II. Front gallery. Restoration is complete except for oak graining the front door.

Fig. 5. Ground floor restored, showing the Creole construction: stuccoed brick walls, brick floors, and the ceiling of exposed dressed joist and floor boards. The sprinkler pipes are visible at ceiling level. The exterior colors are carried through most of the ground floor. *Miller photograph.*

Late in 1974, and before any restoration work was attempted, paint research was begun to determine the original colors. Professional paint analysts using special equipment exposed and recorded all layers of paint from samples taken in several hundred locations. The color, soil, and wear on each layer of paint were noted, and important colors were coded by the Munsell system. Removing any paint before recording the layers is a disaster for a restoration. On the contrary, the more layers of paint that encrust a building the better, for by analyzing the layers one can not only determine the original colors but verify later additions to a building, or help authenticate a puzzling architectural detail.

At San Francisco the paint analysis was fairly complex. We had decided to restore the house to the period of the decorated ceilings, regardless of their date. The analysis revealed that originally the major rooms had been wallpapered and the ceilings and trim painted light colors. Soon thereafter walls had been painted bold colors, five of the ceilings decorated, and some of the trim grained and marbled. Lacking records, we have been unable to date this work exactly. Stylistically it could have been done between the late 1850's and about 1870, but we feel that economic conditions during or right after the Civil War would have made such a redecoration unlikely. In our opinion Antoine Valsin and Louise Marmillion redecorated the house in the late 1850's or early 1860's, about the time the name St. Frusquin first appears.[6]

Unfortunately, the testing laboratory could not come up with a technique to remove the overpainting from those decorated ceilings which had been covered. A ground coat had been applied over a soft first coat of paint. The decoration had then been painted on and, probably when it began to flake, a hard coat of overpainting had locked

Fig. 6. Parlor at the left of the entry hall before restoration (see also Pl. III, Fig. 7). The typical Creole mantel and French doors were old fashioned by the time the house was built. The capitals of the columns are cast iron and are marked J. L. JACKSON./NEW-YORK.

Fig. 7. Main-floor entry hall looking toward the parlor shown in Fig. 6. The original fixed panels have been replaced behind the columns, and the parlor ceiling and marbling of the mantel and baseboards have been restored. *Miller photograph.*

it in. Drawings of the designs were made directly on the ceilings (Fig. 8), which were photographed, and the basic colors were identified.

By early 1975 the paint analysis was under way, the archaeologists were at work on the site, and we were able to start opening up the building and removing later work. We began by looking at some obvious problems, starting with the center back room on the main, or second, floor. In old Creole practice this would have been an open loggia with a small room at each end. But we found that the exterior wall was original. It is a four-inch-thick, brick-between-post wall, stuccoed outside and plastered inside. The posts are exposed on the outside and an applied molding covers the joint between wood and stucco (see Fig. 3).

The ground floor of the building had been most altered. Regularly spaced vertical cracks in the exterior walls of the front corner rooms on that floor suggested that the masonry between the uprights was not original but had been filled in after the building was completed. This indeed proved to be the case, for the original exterior stucco and paint were found on all sides of the uprights. When the masonry was removed, the front rooms at the right and left corners vanished.

When we first came to the house, access to the two rooms at the back corners of the ground floor was gained by doors from the back center room. However, on the frames of these doors we found none of the earliest coats of paint and on the back of one was penciled *Achille Bougère*. Once the sequences of paint layers had been recorded we removed the stucco from the walls of those corner rooms and discovered that both rooms had originally opened toward the front of the house, not into the back center room. The ground-floor corner room labeled "stores" in Figure 1 contained two large earthenware jars set deeply into the floor, a wrought-iron plumbing trap connected to a lead drainpipe, and evidence of a partition wall. This room originally opened into a room which had plugs set at regular intervals into the masonry walls. These plugs were covered with layers of the earliest paint and were spaced as would be required for wall-mounted cabinets. The other back corner room on the ground floor, clearly a wine cellar, had iron bars but no glazed sash in the window frames. Still in the room were a wine rack and a crudely made table, presumably for drying wine bottles. The wine cellar originally opened into what appears to have

been a rather finely finished room.

Later wooden ceilings were removed on the ground floor to reveal the original old Creole-style exposed-joist and floor-board construction and significant runs of handmade lead plumbing pipes, all bearing the earliest paint sequences (see Fig. 5). Some of the original herringbone-pattern brick paving remained, and our investigations showed that the ground-floor room now called the dining room originally had a painted and waxed plaster floor.

It was in the ground-floor center back room that, as architects, we encountered the most painful test of our rule of strictly adhering to the evidence provided by the building. We found that it had originally been an open loggia with square supporting piers like those on the front of the house. The arched door and the first two windows on either side of it were later inserted between the columns. Unhappily, however, the initials *E B M* were painted on the frame

Fig. 8. Detail of the parlor to the right of the entry. The designs of the decorated ceiling have been drawn on the overpainting for later restoration. (The ceiling has since been restored.) The cornices in the house are unusual. In some of the back rooms they are grained to resemble fiddleback maple on the convex moldings and bird's-eye maple on the concave moldings. The effect is remarkably three dimensional.

Pl. III.   Ceiling of the parlor at the left of the entry hall before restoration (see also Fig. 6).

of the door, showing that the loggia had been closed in by the original builder, who had changed his mind, possibly because the loggia made the house too cold, insufficiently private, or both. But we did leave the wall open for some months and admired the first concept.

The plan of the house became simpler as we stripped away later additions. What we think took place is that the Bougères, with a larger family than the Marmillions, added the two rooms on the ground floor at the front and thus changed the character of the building. Essentially, the original ground floor was in the old Creole style: a fine dining room with service rooms surrounding it. From the paint sequence on the main floor, we were able to verify that this plan of the ground floor was true to the period of the painted ceilings.

Once the original fabric and design of the house were established repair work started with the roof. Both gray and greenish-purple slates were found in the attic. By examining these slates and nail holes in the roof sheathing, the archaeologists were able to say that the spacing of the

older nailing matched the spacing of the holes in the gray, not the purple, slates. The framing of the roof was strengthened with tie rods and extra wooden beams and posts. Chimneys and belvedere railings were restored from surviving fragments and on the evidence of old photographs. Certain major beams at the ground-floor level were judged to be too small for their load, and several other beams and some posts had rotted. All had to be replaced. The entire balcony outside the attic and the main cornice were repaired and made as level as possible. The beam supporting the front porch had joints in structurally bad locations and was tied together.

Every effort was made to use the best and most appropriate materials so as to minimize future maintenance. Heart mahogany was used for the millwork, and structural repairs were made with wood treated against rot and wood borers. A moisture-resistant chemical was used on all new wood. Some of the brackets at the attic level and the

Pl. IV. *Left and below:* Bedroom door and detail showing its lower right-hand panel. The rails and stiles were originally light blue and the trim was picked out with blue lines. The ceiling of this bedroom is painted with a vine-hung lattice and three Negro *putti* in a roundel in the center. *Above:* A panel from one of the right-hand parlor's doors.

newels, balusters, and rail of the front stair were cast in polyester from surviving wooden fragments. Masonry and stucco repairs were made with hand-mixed mortar, old, soft brick, and hand-mixed lime paint so that the new work would bond with the old and would be equally elastic and porous.

The roof-drainage system was rebuilt, for getting rid of rain water quickly is essential in a Louisiana building. It is equally important to maintain some moisture in the masonry walls to keep the bricks and mortar from drying out and crumbling.

When the exterior had been restored, work on the interior began. Based on evidence in the house, we were sure that the large doors and fixed panels of the main-floor entry hall were original, and we restored them. The missing second interior stair was easily duplicated from the one still in place. On the ground floor the brick floors were relaid, the walls restuccoed, and missing millwork restored—all based on clear evidence in the fabric of the building.

An example of the way we proceeded is the restoration of the interior French doors on the ground floor. In the French manner pairs of doors with glass lights above and wooden panels below were used not only on the exterior, but on the interior. Consistent with Creole tradition, the

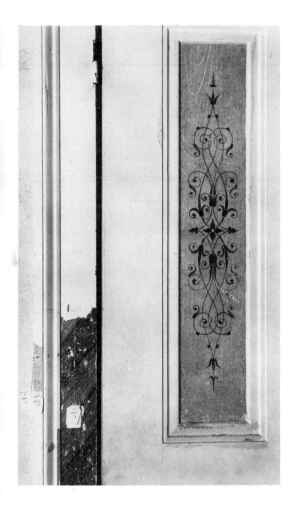

Fig. 9. Detail of a bedroom door. Scraping revealed the grained doorframe and decorated panels. In this room the overpainting could be scraped off fairly easily and most of the original painted decoration had only to be touched up.

Fig. 10. Much of the millwork in the house bears the painted initials *EBM* for Edmond Bozonier Marmillion. The board bearing the initials *VB* (presumably for Valsin Bozonier [Marmillion]) was found inside a ground-floor closet at the base of one of the chimneys. As the closet opens to the outdoors, we suspect that it was a storeroom for boots and other outdoor gear.

exterior doors on the ground floor had their original French doors set behind solid-wood blinds. The question arose as to whether the ground-floor interior doors at San Francisco also had these solid blinds—not an unusual occurrence in old Creole buildings. The dining-room doors had the key to the answer. Of the six dining-room doors we found in 1974, only three appeared to be original. Of these, two opened out and the center exterior door opened into the room. The latter was protected by a solid-wood shutter, the only such shutter on any of the dining-room doors. The paint sequences told us that in the beginning all three original doors had opened into the room. We then found two other doors of the right design and color sequence for the dining room in the two front corner rooms that the Bougères had added on the ground floor. We concluded that all six dining-room doors had originally opened into the room and that all had had solid-wood blinds. Our analysis of the paint layers under the bolts which secured the doors showed that at the same time the Bougères created the two front corner rooms on the ground floor they removed the blinds from what then became five (not three) interior doors to the dining room, and rehung the five pairs of French doors so that they opened out of the room. Only the single exterior dining-room door continued to open inward and retained its wooden blind. In our restoration we reset all the doors so that they opened inward and we installed six sets of wooden blinds.

Similar archaeological research at the house established that the exterior stairs consisted of original masonry piers and lattice, and that the handrail was similar to the railing around the belvedere. Both railings were undoubtedly installed by the Bougères and they are the only parts of the restored building that date from the second owners' time. We have left them even though they are inconsistent in scale and design. Without evidence of the original railings we felt it inappropriate to invent something.

In some places we were forced to invent. Based on extensive research we carried out for the Gallier House several years ago, we designed millwork for the food storeroom and pantry. The Gothic revival lights in the doors of the pantry cabinets repeat motifs found on the exterior of the house, but they are also not without local precedent. The food-storage bins and lattice partition in the restored storeroom are based on existing millwork found locally. However, we do not pretend that they are anything but educated guesses.

How ducts, pipes, and wires are installed in an old building is determined by the nature of the building and the budget. The masonry construction of the ground floor, the open-beam ceiling, and the main-floor walls built of posts filled in solidly with brick imposed difficult conditions, as we did not choose to cut out original structural timbers to accommodate the services. By partitioning one end of the wine cellar and using what was originally a closet above, it was possible to run pipes and conduit to the attic, where the main heating and air-conditioning, sprinkler, and electrical equipment is housed. Wiring on the main floor is enclosed in metal conduit that is set into the floor boards, a technique made possible by the nineteenth-century taste for wall-to-wall coverings: the carpets have hidden the conduit. Wiring on the ground floor, also enclosed in metal conduit, is set into the masonry walls. The house is illuminated by electrified oil lamps and electric candles. Care has been taken to use only as many fixtures as were typical of the period so that the level of light is the same as it was in the 1860's.

Fig. 11. San Francisco in a photograph taken between 1879 (when the Bougères bought the plantation) and 1896. In 1876 the riverbank at average low water was seven hundred feet from the house; by 1896 it was only three hundred and eighty feet away, and subsequently it moved closer still. *Photograph by courtesy of L. N. Bougère.*

Extensive paint scraping was done on the interior to reveal as much of the original graining and marbling as possible. In two rooms the paint on the doors and windows and their frames, the baseboards, and a mantel is almost entirely original. A patch of nearly every kind of graining or marbling throughout the house has been kept as a record next to restored areas. The decorated ceilings have been cleaned, touched up, or repainted much as an oil painting is restored.

A photograph taken before 1896 shows an extraordinary formal garden in front of the house (Fig. 11). Had not the levee twice been moved back so that it is now almost at the house, the restoration of the garden would undoubtedly have been recommended.

There is a strong feeling today that a historic building is best preserved by showing all evidence of the changes that have taken place through the years. Without going into this very complex and important subject, I believe that each building must be handled as a separate case. There is no doubt that this house could have been preserved as of the later nineteenth century, the early twentieth century, or as of 1973. However, we have preferred to restore the unique, rather flamboyant character of the house when it was owned by the Marmillions and was called St. Frusquin.

---

[1] An important Louisiana inventor and engineer of the early nineteenth century, and a pioneer in the development of machinery for sugar mills, was a free man of color named Norbert Rillieux, but we do not know his relationship, if any, to Elisée.

[2] E. B. Marmillion's estate paid some bills for construction in 1856 and 1857, but whether for the house or the sugar mill is not known.

[3] Louise Marmillion and her three daughters died and were buried in Germany. Her death notice in the New Orleans *Times Democrat* for February 7, 1904, gives her maiden name as Von Seybold.

[4] In 1880 the son of Pierre Edmond Marmillion was the plantation manager for Bougère, and there was a German gardener in residence, according to the United States census for that year.

[5] The following companies and individuals have been involved in the restoration of San Francisco:

Owners	San Francisco Plantation Foundation: G. Glen Martin, president of the board of trustees
Financial support	Marathon Oil Company: Harold D. Hoopman, president and chief executive officer; Charles H. Barré, vice president of refining
	Ingram Corporation
	Northeast Petroleum Industries
Owners' administrative consultant	Gallier House: Nadine C. Russell, director-curator
Architects	Koch and Wilson, Architects: Samuel Wilson Jr., Henry W. Krotzer Jr., Barry M. Fox

Interior design	Henry A. Dornsife and Sons: Samuel J. Dornsife
Structural engineer	Neill Jeffrey and Associates
Mechanical and electrical engineer	Joseph E. Leininger and Associates
General contractor	Haase Construction Company, Incorporated: Robert R. Haase, president; James Sones, project superintendent
Subcontractors	
Mechanical and electrical	Comfortair Company, Incorporated
Painting	Frank J. Matthew Company, Incorporated
Millwork	Alex J. Kondroik Millwork Company, Incorporated
	Architectural Wood Manufacturers
Sprinkler system	American Sprinkler Company, Incorporated
Fire-detecting system	Delta Safety and Supply Company, Incorporated
Security system	ADF Services
Roofing contractor	Standard Company of New Orleans, Incorporated
Archaeology—subgrade	Department of Anthropology, University of New Orleans: J. Richard Shenkel
Restoration of painted decoration	Campbell, Smith and Company, Limited
Graining and marbling	Robson Worldwide Graining

[6] The redecoration could have been financed by the bumper sugar-cane crops of 1858-1859 and 1861-1862.

The John Wornall House, Kansas City, Missouri

BY KATHLEEN NELSON TAGGART, *Research historian for the Wornall House*

THE GREEK REVIVAL house built by John Bristow Wornall in 1858 in Kansas City, Missouri, reflects the Kentucky plantation style which in the mid-nineteenth century shaped Missouri's architecture (Pl. I). This is hardly surprising, since in the Jackson County, Missouri, censuses of 1850 and 1860 by far the largest number of residents listed Kentucky as their place of origin. Along the Missouri River white-porticoed brick mansions still punctuate the rolling landscape and are clustered in towns with Kentucky names such as Lexington, Liberty, Glasgow, and Independence. Before the Civil War many such houses were built in the

Fig. 1. The façade of the John Wornall House (Pl. I) follows the Kentucky Greek revival pattern. The house is L shape, with two parlors and two bedrooms in the front, and dining room, kitchen, and two more bedrooms in the two-story ell. *Photographs are by Helga Photo Studio.*

newly incorporated City of Kansas, as Kansas City was first called, and in the nearby town of Westport (now part of Kansas City), but the Wornall House is one of the few that remain today within the city limits.

In 1843 John Wornall's father migrated with his family and slaves from Shelbyville, Kentucky, to a site near Westport, Missouri. They settled in a small frame house on a five-hundred-acre farm that the elder Wornall purchased from Isaac and John McCoy. When his wife died in 1849, the elder Wornall moved back to Kentucky, leaving the farm to his son John, then twenty-seven. Wheat from the farm found a ready market in the small town of Westport, where wagon trains were outfitted for trips west and south. John Wornall brought his second wife, the eighteen-year-old Eliza Johnson, to the farm in 1854. She was the daughter of a prominent Methodist missionary who ran a school for the Shawnee Indians in the neighboring Kansas Territory.

By 1858 Wornall was ready to build a new house for his growing family. The story of its construction was recalled half a century later by one of his workmen:

My host referred me to a well-to-do farmer, a true gentleman regarded by everybody as one of the best and leading citizens. . . . When I came to him Mr. Wornald was living in a comfortable house but soon determined to build a two story brick mansion which would be the most pretentious of anything in that section. I continued to work on his farm . . . at $15 a month . . . until he commenced assembling material for his proposed mansion, then I was assigned to hauling sand from a sandbank on the Missouri River seven miles distant, several blocks below Main Street, Kansas City, with a four-mule team, while other hands were employed in hauling brick from a kiln and other material near by. When the material was assembled I helped to carry the brick and mortar to put up the building, a good, substantial structure that stood the storms of war and time. . . .''[1]

No contemporary record has been found naming an architect of the house. The balanced façade with projecting two-story portico (Fig. 1), an L-shape plan, high-ceilinged rooms, and open side galleries (Fig. 2) are all features of the Greek revival houses of Kentucky. Family correspondence indicates that the Wornalls maintained contact with their friends in Kentucky, and it seems probable that John Wornall returned to Shelby County before marrying his first wife, Matilda Polk of Taylorsville (a town near Shelbyville), in 1850. This marriage ended with Matilda's death in 1851. Wornall clearly knew Woodlawn, Montrose, and the Bird family house (all extant private houses in Shelbyville), for they closely resemble his own. The Bird and Wornall houses have very similar interior woodwork.

Documents in the Wornall House make it possible to fill in many details about its construction. In May 1858 Wornall paid $211 for laths and shingles; in July, $22 for the "forty brackets" under the eaves; and in August a Westport merchant supplied gutters, cistern heads, locks, and latches. The builders Bright and Royster of Westport acknowledged a first payment of $200 on August 28; by mid-November the entire cost of $981 had been paid. The charge for carpentry stipulated in the contract was $800, but, as always, there were extras:

Pl. I. John Wornall House, Kansas City, Missouri, built in 1858 by John Wornall (1822-1892). It is listed in the Historic American Buildings Survey and the National Register. The Jackson County Historical Society bought the house from descendants of the builder and now operates it as a museum. Federal grants, in addition to funds raised by the historical society, made possible the restoration of the house. The architect in charge of the restoration was John A. Huffman. Furnishings given by many individuals and organizations were selected with help from the curatorial staffs of local museums.

To Building Smo House	50.00
`` Getting out Extra Trims	40.00
`` 7 Door frames Extra	14.00
`` 4 Window `` Do	8.00
`` 1 Stair Way & Door in Cellar	10.00
`` 1 Extra press under Stairway	6.00
`` 1 Petition in backroom on Porch & Shelving	12.00
`` Extra in Columns of Size	6.00
`` Turning Muelpost & cap	1.50

Additional charges were also made for handrail screws, sash cords, and a "door lift," among other items. The mantel in the main parlor cost $7 extra, the mantel in the second parlor was $5 extra, and three other mantels, apparently in two bedrooms and the kitchen, cost a total of $6. The "Muelpost" cited above and the handrail of the front stair are of walnut, and a paneled wall conceals the "Extra press under Stairway." Family papers also tell us that after the completion of the house Wornall paid part of his doctor's bill in surplus brick.

Fig. 2. Doors opening on the south galleries provide cross ventilation for the front hall, dining room, kitchen, and two bedrooms in the ell. The only route from the dining room to the kitchen is along the gallery. The only access to the two bedrooms upstairs in the ell is by the gallery stair.

Fig. 3. The kitchen fireplace is fitted with a crane for cooking, although the nearby smokehouse undoubtedly contained a summer kitchen as well. According to tradition Mrs. Wornall prepared breakfast here for both Union and Confederate soldiers before the Battle of Westport, which took place on October 23, 1864. The house was used as a hospital for the wounded of both sides during the battle. The Wornall kitchen is now the site of classes for children, to demonstrate cooking on the hearth in the Southern manner, and to explain the modern conveniences of the 1860's, such as the coffee mill, apple corer, cherry seeder, patent spice boxes, and flytrap.

Fig. 4. Another view of the kitchen. The 1836 map shows the United States to its westernmost border at the Missouri River. The crude walnut cupboard was made in Missouri. Wornall bills for kitchen equipment in the 1850's and 1860's include a cookbook, brass kettle, brass candlestick, ''Jap'd. candlestick,'' ''Pattent Ballances,'' pie dish, wash tub, washboard, coffee mill, brooms, stoneware jars, palm fan, three dozen candles, matches, butcher knife, and a rattrap. Staples purchased included coffee, tea, soda, salt, rice, flour, sugar, molasses, syrup, raisins, citron, a kit (tub) of mackerel, a can of oysters, a pint of brandy ($1), and its bottle (fifteen cents). These quarterly bills were usually paid in hams, lard, quarters of beef, bacon, tallow, or the use of a yoke of oxen.

Fig 5 Dining-room furniture from the mid-nineteenth century Kansas City farmhouse of the Marcus Gill and Allen B. H. McGee families includes the mahogany table with twin vase-shape pedestals, and chairs with vase-shape splats. The Gill-McGee furniture was donated by Mr. and Mrs. Webster W. Townley. The walnut high chair is from Philadelphia and the cherry sugar chest from Kentucky. Between the first and second shelves of the cupboard is the window to the kitchen through which dishes of food were passed. The room was heated by a small stove. The cast-iron Young America No. 1 stove visible through the door in Pl. II was patented in 1853 by J. C. Fletcher and Company and was manufactured by Bridge and Brothers of St. Louis. It is on loan from the Kansas City Museum of Science and History.

In the Kentucky Greek revival tradition, the façade of the house is unusually imposing, with its brick pilasters, balcony with cast-iron railing over the front door, and the outsize columns noted above as a $6 extra.

A small opening in the dining-room cupboard (Fig. 5) gave servants access to the kitchen (Figs. 3, 4), for originally there was no door between the two rooms. The two back bedrooms can only be reached by the gallery stair shown in Figure 2. The service buildings at the back of the house included a smokehouse and an icehouse, both of which were still standing as late as 1910, as well as slave cabins, barns, and other outbuildings.

When the Wornall House was sold by direct descendants of the builder to the Jackson County Historical Society in 1964, a minimum of work was needed to restore it to its appearance in the late 1850's and early 1860's. Structurally this involved reopening the south galleries which had been glassed in as sun porches, replacing existing mantels with wooden ones (although not with the original ones, which had vanished), reconstructing the opening to the kitchen in the dining-room cupboard, opening up the kitchen fireplace, and dismantling a modern kitchen. Worn but usable random-width pine flooring was salvaged from the ground-

floor rooms for use in the upper rooms, hearths were returned to their original depth, and the original brick-red and ginger-brown paint colors were duplicated in the second parlor (Pl. II) and dining room (Figs. 5, 6). The restoration was completed and the house was opened to the public in 1972.

Original family furniture remaining in the house included the square Steinway piano in the main parlor and two low upholstered chairs, which are also in the parlor (Fig. 7). Almost as soon as the house was completed, in November 1858, the Wornalls purchased a stove for $9, perhaps to warm the dining room, which had no fireplace. Within a year the Westport cabinetmaker Henry Sager, who had advertised that he could make anything to order, supplied a sofa for $25, a ''country table'' for $16, and a ''secre-taire[?] table'' for $18. The same bill also lists beehives, a ''trunel bedsted and mattrass,'' and two small ''coffin boxes with trimmings.''

Advertisements in the *Westport Border Star* indicate that almost anything available on the East Coast could reach Westport by boat from St. Louis and New Orleans. J. and

Pl. II. Less formal than the parlor across the front hall, this cheerful second parlor with reproduction Rose Damask wallpaper was the center of family life. A fire of walnut logs burned constantly; the fireplace is lined with stone rather than the brick used in the main parlor; the hearth projects deep into the pine-floored room. The clock on the mantel has works by Oliver Weldon of Bristol, Connecticut. The desk-and-bookcase is of a type familiar in Missouri. It was shipped by riverboat from Kentucky to Independence, then carried by oxcart to Lee's Summit, a town not far from Kansas City.

P. Shannon's Dry Goods on the northeast corner of Main and Front streets in Westport carried notices of shipments from New York and abroad of upholstery, marseilles and Lancaster counterpanes, dress fabrics of every sort, and, in one case, ''100 pieces of elegant and superb carpet—Brussels, 3 ply, tapestry, ingrain, felt, hemp and stair—all of this year's manufacture.''[2] The brightly flowered Wilton-type carpet now in the main parlor (Fig. 7) is woven in twenty-seven-inch strips. It contrasts with the cool gray walls and white woodwork.

Pl. III. North front bedroom. The walnut bed and chest of drawers were made by Mitchell and Rammelsberg of Cincinnati, in 1859 and 1858 respectively. The dated trapunto quilt was completed in 1859 by America Aingell Tully of Harmony Hall, near Russellville, Kentucky. The walnut rocker descended in the Wornall family.

Wherever possible contemporary records have guided the furnishing of the restored house. American Empire furniture as well as pieces in the more up-to-date rococo revival style have been used. Many are gifts from other early Kansas City families.

An important document in the Wornall House papers is a receipt for $1 postage on the "Ladies Book, July 1859-July 1860." Eliza Wornall was by no means exceptional in having Godey's publication sent from Philadelphia, since the monthly magazine contains notices of appreciation from ladies as far away as Oregon, California, and Alabama. Readers were kept abreast of the latest news in fashion, furniture, and modern inventions, and were wisely guided by Sarah Josepha Hale's editorial advice on the furnishing and care of the house. Her column, "Center Table Gossip," as well as numerous illustrations in the *Lady's Book* indicate the importance of the Empire pedestal table in what she termed the "common family room," which was the scene of lessons, Bible readings, and sewing (Pl. II).

Long semiannual bills from the Westport dry-goods firm of Street and Baker to the Wornalls testify to the prodigious amount of sewing carried out for family and slaves. A silk or poplin dress pattern, shirt bosoms and sleeves, "Swiss flouncing," as well as "negro goods," "Kentucky jean," and blue drill, and yards of ribbon and lace were fashioned into garments to be worn with a store-bought satin vest, fur cloak, morocco leather boots, or "casconett pants." The fashionably dressed Wornall family rode to church in a four-wheeled carriage of the type known as a rockaway, and entertained on "dining days" when their friends from Westport or neighboring farms came at noon to enjoy their bountiful hospitality. At night both candles and deodorized coal oil provided illumination.

The two front bedrooms have been furnished in contrasting styles. The south bedroom (Fig. 8) suggests furniture that the Wornalls might have inherited. In his will John Wornall's grandfather, for example, left each child land, a horse, and "one bedstead and furniture." The tall walnut wardrobe, a Wornall family piece, is identical to one that belonged to Eliza Wornall's father, Thomas Johnson, and which is now exhibited at the Shawnee Methodist Mission and Indian Manual Labor School in Shawnee Mission, Kansas.

The north bedroom (Pl. III), restored as a gift of the Society of Colonial Dames of America in Kansas City, is furnished with fashionable rococo revival pieces of the kind that might have been purchased in 1858 or 1859 for the large new house. The walnut bed and chest of drawers surmounted by a kidney-shape looking glass were both manufactured by Mitchell and Rammelsberg, a very important Cincinnati firm whose elaborate work is just beginning to be identified in Missouri, Kansas, Iowa, and other Midwestern states. The chest of drawers is stenciled with their Cincinnati address for the year 1858; the bed bears the stencil of their St. Louis showroom, which was opened in 1859. Thomas Johnson owned an identical chest of drawers and a matching commode, which are both now at the Shawnee Methodist Mission.

Fig. 6. The fine mahogany sideboard of c. 1825 was brought to Howard County, Missouri, from Virginia. The design for the curtains follows a pattern in *Godey's Lady's Book* of June 1860. The six-piece silver-plated tea set by Rogers, Smith and Company of Waterbury, Connecticut, on the sideboard is very similar to one illustrated in the 1856 catalogue of E. Jaccard and Company of St. Louis.

[1] Wiley Britton, "Pioneer Life in Southwest Missouri," *Missouri Historical Review*, vol. 16 (April 1922), pp. 416-421.

[2] *Westport Border Star*, December 31, 1858.

Fig. 7.   In the main parlor gold-color curtains banded in green are set within the pedimented Greek revival window frames with projecting ears. In the *Westport Border Star* for May 26, 1860, Shannon's store on the levee in Westport advertised "cornish gimp and tassels." In *Godey's Lady's Book* for June of the same year it was noted that "a pair of tassels hanging from a rope in the center . . . will be found to look well from the outside of the house as well as from the room." The Steinway piano, patented in 1859, and the upholstered chair are Wornall family pieces. The portrait above the mantel is attributed to George Caleb Bingham (1811-1879) and depicts Christina Polk McCoy, from whose husband and son the Wornalls bought their land.

Fig. 8.   South front bedroom. The walnut wardrobe is a Wornall family piece and the walnut trundle bed probably resembles the "trunel bedsted and mattrass" for which Wornall was billed $8 in 1859 by Henry Sager, a Westport cabinetmaker. The colored lithographs of *Summer* and *Autumn* are from a set of the Four Seasons published in 1853 by Goupil et Compagnie of Paris for M. Knoedler of New York City.

Olana—the artist as architect

BY PETER L. GOSS, *Assistant professor, Graduate School of Architecture, University of Utah*

PERHAPS THE FINEST of the few surviving eclectic picturesque villas in America is Olana, the home of Frederic Edwin Church, the Hudson River school painter. Located on a bluff on the east bank of the Hudson River, Olana commands magnificent views of the Hudson River valley and the Taconic, Berkshire, and Catskill mountain ranges, and is across the river from Catskill, New York, the home of Church's mentor, Thomas Cole. Virtually unchanged since the nineteenth century, the site, comprising over several hundred acres, remained in the Church family until shortly before its acquisition by the state of New York in 1966.[1] Olana represents one of Church's greatest attempts to attain perfection. This goal, which he sought in his panoramic landscape paintings, became almost an obsession as he strove over a thirty-year period to orchestrate the architecture of the house and its furnishings with the landscaping of the site.[2]

Church was the son of a successful Hartford, Connecticut, businessman. He showed an aptitude for drawing at an early age and in 1844, with the financial support of his father, he began two years of formal study with Thomas Cole at Catskill. Church rapidly achieved success as a painter and was elected a full member of the National Academy of Design in 1849. In the following decade he produced *Niagara* (1857), one of his most famous paintings, and traveled twice to South America, influenced, in part, by the writings of Baron Alexander von Humboldt (1769-1859). While there Church made sufficient sketches to serve as the basis for many later paintings. The largest and grandest of these, *The Heart of the Andes*, was completed in 1859. Financially Church became one of the most successful artists of the third quarter of the nineteenth century, and his panoramic landscapes, often of an exotic nature, attracted not only the critics' praise but also great crowds to their public viewings. This active career, combining travel with months of work in his Tenth Street studio,[3] continued well into the next decade, when Church and his wife set sail for Europe and the Middle East in November 1867.

In 1860 Church married Isabel M. Carnes and soon after, they moved into a newly constructed rural-style cottage believed to have been designed by Richard Morris Hunt. (The cottage was on land that is part of Olana today.[4]) Shortly before their trip in 1867 Church commissioned Hunt to design a larger house. The architect drew up plans for a French-chateau-style estate to be located on a prominent site overlooking a body of water, presumably the Hudson River. However, the artist's trip to Europe and the Middle East changed his thoughts on architecture.

Abroad for more than a year and a half, Church seemed unimpressed with much of what he experienced in Europe. He was, however, enthralled with the eastern Mediterranean and the remains of its ancient civilizations. In addition to the major European capitals, he also visited Jerusalem, Beirut, Petra, Baalbek, and Constantinople. The trip became a dominant influence in Church's later painting career, and stimulated his desire to build a large dwelling in the Eastern manner on his property along the Hudson.

In letters, sketches, and diaries Church and his wife made extensive comments about the architecture of the Middle East. Writing to his friends Erastus Dow Palmer, the sculptor, and William Henry Osborn, a director of the

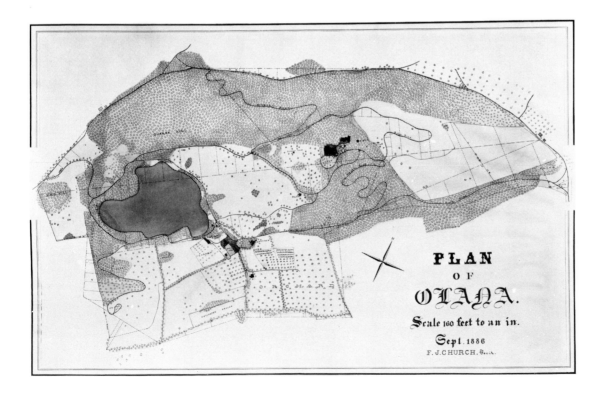

Fig. 1. Map of the Olana estate drawn by Church's son Frederic J. in September 1886.

74

Illinois Central Railroad, Church enthusiastically described the Eastern central-court houses and their construction. Diary entries by Isabel Church carefully noted the architecture of several houses in Damascus, particularly their ornate decoration.

Excited by all he had experienced, and armed with many ideas on construction, Church wrote to Osborn, ''sometimes the desire to build attacks man like a fever—and at it he rushes.''[5] Shortly after returning home in the summer of 1869 Church decided to break ground for his new house. He engaged the architectural firm of Vaux, Withers and Company regarding a design. In consultation with the architects a plan was agreed upon and construction began in 1870.

Pl. I. Olana, the eclectic picturesque villa of the Hudson River school painter Frederic Edwin Church (1826-1900). Begun in 1870, the house was designed by the artist in consultation with architects Calvert Vaux (1824-1895) and Frederick Clarke Withers (1828-1901). The studio wing, at the left, was built between 1888 and 1891. *Photographs are by Helga Photo Studio.*

Calvert Vaux, once an assistant to the landscape architect Andrew Jackson Downing, was then a popular architect and well known for his house-pattern book *Villas and Cottages* (1857). Vaux submitted several plans and elevations to Church and evident in each, most likely at Church's insistence, were a central court with a stairway to one side, and a dining room/picture gallery with high ceilings.[6] The cruciform central court was to be enclosed overhead due

to the climate. The dining room/picture gallery was to be hung with the artist's collection of old-master paintings accumulated abroad, and the upper walls were to be decorated with frescoes, since Church had mastered the technique while in Rome.[7]

Once the ground-floor plan was satisfactorily established, Church took over the design of the house, consulting with Vaux and Withers during the trying moments of the construction. Undoubtedly, they had some influence on the evolution of Church's design but the architectural massing of Olana was totally changed from the elevations provided

Fig. 3. The loggia, part of the studio wing, has unusually shaped columns that were inspired by columns seen in Isfahan, Iran.

Fig. 4. All the furniture in the northeast corner of the east parlor was arranged according to old family photographs. Above the desk is a field study of a sunset in Jamaica by Church, and the large painting of an autumnal scene on the left originally hung in Church's parents' house in Hartford, Connecticut. The oil sketch above it is believed to be of a place in Germany.

by the architects. Church proudly stated in a letter to a friend, "I am building a house and am principally my own architect. I give directions all day and draw plans and working drawings all night."[8]

During the construction Church was in constant communication with Erastus Dow Palmer, who was once a carpenter, and he relied on his friend for advice on such practical matters as labor and materials. By late summer of 1872 the family was able to move in, although a fair amount of the exterior and interior detail and decoration was not finished for many years.

Included in Church's early designs are drawings of façades incorporating both Renaissance and Gothic motifs. These were quickly abandoned in favor of another series of watercolor elevations. He even built a crude model of the house, painting the details of the east façade in oils. All of Church's final elevations are richer in color, material, and surface decoration than the over-all perspective furnished earlier by Vaux and Withers. He continued to refine and redraw portions and details of the exterior, frequently providing two or more alternatives from which he and Mrs. Church might choose (see Pls. VIII, IX). His correspondence with Palmer and other friends indicates that certain details were completed just prior to their execution by his workmen.

This approach to the design of the façade was also used for the interior decoration. Pencil and watercolor sketches for the woodwork of the main staircase and small stencil patterns are numerous; color schemes for the walls and stenciled borders of the many rooms were crudely painted in oils on cardboard. Church worked intermittently on details of the interior into the mid-1880's and superintended all this work as he did the construction.

Designs based largely on "Muslim"[9] architecture appeared in nineteenth-century house-pattern books but few such structures were ever built. The difficulty with the designs, claimed Calvert Vaux in *Villas and Cottages,* was primarily the expense of construction and decoration. Two notable American examples of this style preceded Olana. The earliest was P. T. Barnum's Iranistan, near Bridgeport, Connecticut, which burned a decade after it was built. The second was Longwood, also referred to as "Nutt's folly," begun in 1860 near Natchez, Mississippi, which today remains unfinished.

Olana, probably named after a place in Persia by Mrs. Church some years after its completion, was claimed by her to be "Persian adopted to the Occident."[10] Its affinity to Persian architecture is most obvious in the concentration of colorful decorative elements on parts of the façades as well as the ornately painted and stenciled interiors. However, the architectural massing of Olana is similar to the picturesque Italian-villa style as exemplified in Richard Upjohn's 1845 design for the Edward King residence in Newport, Rhode Island.

Consciously striving for visual effect, Church used a wide range of materials and colors on the façades, each of which is different. The rough quarry-face stone of the walls contrasting with the fine-cut stone of the drip caps, moldings, and sills is combined with polychromed brick, glazed Persian and Mexican tiles, and wooden decoration. Polychromed towers and chimneys projecting from the roof line give an irregular silhouette. The veranda (prior to the addition of the studio wing), the bay windows, the porch, the ombra,[11] and the recessed portions of the façades were inherited from Vaux and Withers and achieved a necessary variety of light and shade. Their arrangement evolved in a manner similar to that in which Church painted landscapes: assembling and drawing inspiration from sketches he made abroad, numerous books on eastern architecture and decoration, and photographs of Persia, North Africa, and India.

The interior decoration of Olana must have consumed a good deal of Church's energy, considering the many extant sketches for stairs, doors, fireplaces, windows, and the over-all appearance of each room. Walls were painted colors determined beforehand in oil sketches and were bordered with colorful arabesque stencils derived from Church's collection of works on Persian and Arabic decoration. He purchased numerous "Persian" *objets d'art*, including fireplaces, rugs, brassware, and other antiques from New York importers. He also ordered objects carved

Pl. II. The main entrance is the focal point of the east façade and is the most Persian of Olana's exterior features. The tile patterns and the predominant use of blue are reminiscent of decoration on a mosque entrance or Persian city gate.

Pl. III. The corner tower, to the left of the entrance on the east façade, has a parlor on the main floor, Mrs. Church's bedroom on the second, and a porch or observatory on the third floor. To the right of the entrance is the high-ceilinged dining room/picture gallery. The columns on the second floor are part of the loggia off the children's bedrooms.

in India from the well-known designer and artist Lockwood de Forest, Mrs. Church's cousin. In a letter to Erastus Dow Palmer describing some of these purchases, Church stated, "I take some comfort in the fact that I never paid good money for Hawthorn pottery. . . , or for fancy paper for the parlor or for any such reckless waste of legal tenders."[12]

Church, nearing sixty, painted little during the early 1880's due to a rheumatic wrist. Winters were spent in Mexico recuperating and summers at Olana, where Church enthusiastically worked on his estate, building carriage roads and opening up what he called "views" of the house and the surrounding countryside.[13] Some landscape work had begun in the late 1870's with the creation of a small irregularly shaped lake at the southwest end of the estate below the house (see Fig. 1). However, the majority of landscape improvements were not made until the early 1880's.

Church's approach appears to have been the reverse of that employed in his painting and in the design of Olana. Instead he made arrangements in his mind's eye and transferred them directly to the landscape. Church wanted these to be experienced either from a moving carriage or as static, picturesque compositions. After passing through the south gate one enters a wooded area of spruce, pine, oak, hemlock, butternut, and chestnut. Winding northeastward, the road parallels part of the lake shore and, just beyond

Pl. IV.   Visible for miles, the tower at the southeast corner of the villa is capped with carved and stenciled wooden ornament and multicolor roof slates.

Pl. V.   Polychromed bricks decorate the upper two stories of the tower, and Mexican tiles are found in the balustrades of the open porch on the second floor. The wooden balcony projecting from the second-story east window is off Mrs. Church's bedroom. The bell was brought back from Mexico by Church.

Fig. 5. In the dining room/picture gallery is displayed the collection of old masters Church gathered while in Europe during 1868 and 1869. The furniture in this room has been arranged according to old photographs and includes an 1876 reproduction of a Sheraton sofa and the Church family silver on the table.

Fig. 6. Old photograph of the central-court hall. The light coming in from the left is from the ombra (not visible).

Fig. 7. Central-court hall looking east toward the main entrance. The incorrect Arabic inscription over the front door reads "sharufna" and is translated "you have given us the honor." The bookcases were designed by Church, and the tempera painting of Apollo and the muses over the doorway is one of a set of nine originally owned by Church. On the right-hand wall is a sketch of Isabel Church by S. W. Rocuse, who also did the sketch of *Little Mother Hubbard* on the left.

this point, the landscape to the left begins to open onto grassy fields revealing the tower of the house and a portion of its south façade. The fields and roadside were carefully planted with seemingly random groups of maples, spruce, pine, oak, and birch. This series of picturesque "views" of the house in its landscape continues as the road winds up the hill, and glimpses of the south, east, and north façades are seen by the visitor prior to arriving at the front entrance on the east façade (Pls. II, III).[14] Church particularly enjoyed the scene of the south shore of the lake towards Olana and frequently photographed it, catching the reflection of the villa and the landscape in the lake's surface. Crown Hill, a favorite family picnic spot, was a short ride through the woods from the lake, and from this position Church would sketch Olana framed by foreground foliage.

Inside the house, the landscape and "views" are framed by the ombra and tall windows on the ground floor in the

Fig. 8. The painting of the ancient city of Petra over the mantel in the west parlor was done in 1874. The large painting to the right is entitled *Catskill Falls*. Below are *Sunrise* and *Moonrise*. Hanging over the doorway is an oil sketch of Olana in the winter. All the paintings are by Church.

Overleaf:
Pl. VI. The stair hall of the central court is softly illuminated by the yellow glass in the arched window. Colorful stenciling, derived from plates of Eastern ornament, frame the arches above the stair landing. The wooden staircase was designed by Church and made by local craftsmen. Concentrated in the stair hall are some of Church's finest *objets d'art,* including Persian rugs, brassware, armor, and a gold, wood, and gesso Buddha. The marble sculpture under the staircase is by Erastus Dow Palmer (1817-1904) and is entitled *Sleep.*

Pl. VIII. Watercolor and ink sketch by Church for one of the windows in Mrs. Church's bedroom (see Pl. V).

Pl. IX. Church's watercolor sketch for the ornate stencil pattern originally found on the exterior cornice at Olana.

south and east facades. Looking south and west from the master bedrooms on the second floor and from the third-story tower, one is presented with a vast scene, not unlike the panoramic scope of Church's paintings, with the picturesque landscaped estate in the foreground and the Hudson River and Catskill Mountains in the middle and background.

Church never considered abandoning painting despite his failing health and the immense enjoyment he derived from his landscaping activities. Many of his comfortable studio furnishings remained in his New York City studio, which he rarely used in the late 1870's and 1880's. He did equip one of the outbuildings at Olana as a makeshift studio, but apparently this arrangement was unsatisfactory because in the late 1880's Church decided to add a studio wing to the villa. He chose the western side of the house facing the Hudson River and the Catskill Mountains. It offered a magnificent view of the sun setting behind the mountain range, a subject common to many of his paintings. The addition was begun in 1888 without a formal plan and was not completed to Church's liking until 1891.[15]

Constructed of the same materials as the villa, the three-story wing was built on the slope of the site and provided guest rooms on the ground level, a loggia, gallery, and studio on the main floor, and the artist's observatory above the studio. Spatially, the addition extends the east-west axis of the ground-floor plan from the central court and connecting gallery, terminating in the studio with a large window overlooking a semicircular porch and the

Preceding page:
Pl. VII. The southwest corner of the east parlor includes a hand-carved mahogany mantel from the studio of Lockwood de Forest, Mrs. Church's cousin. Over the mantelpiece is a New England scene by Church, and above it is a painting by Arthur Parton (1842-1914), a Hudson, New York, artist. An oil sketch by Church entitled *Orchards at Olana* is over the doorway, and to the left is an oil sketch by Charles de Wolf Brownell (1822-1909) of a palm tree. The white-lacquer and gold-leaf chair in the foreground is Persian.

Pl. X. One of the lithographic plates from a nineteenth-century collection printed in Paris from which Church derived his colorful arabesque stencils.

Fig. 9. The connecting gallery leads into the studio wing. The portrait on the right is of Church, and the hand-carved mahogany balustrade, in the right foreground, is from Lockwood de Forest's studio. The picnic set under the table on the left belonged to Church and his family.

Hudson River. The connecting gallery separates the studio from the main floor. Oriented to take advantage of the north light, the studio also includes a small bathroom and a stairway leading to the observatory where Church liked to make quick pencil and oil sketches of clouds, sunsets, and the landscape. Paintings by fellow artists decorated the wing, as did a hand-carved balustrade from Lockwood de Forest's studio, Persian rugs, a Persian-tile stove, and other Eastern bric-a-brac. Unfortunately, the wing was little used by the artist in the remaining nine years of his life due to the ill health of both him and his wife.

Andrew Jackson Downing claimed that villas should be known for their "originality, boldness, energy, and variety of character" and their owners should be "men of imagination—men whose aspirations never leave them at rest—men whose ambition and energy will give them no peace within the mere bounds of rationality."[16] Olana and Frederic Edwin Church aptly fit these descriptions, and the exotic quality found in Church's large panoramic, idealized paintings of such extremes in subject as Niagara Falls, the tropics, South America, and icebergs in the North Atlantic, is also present in the eclectic use of ornamental and colorful Eastern motifs at Olana. Dominating its hilltop site with projecting towers and polychromed façades, Olana still enjoys a picturesque relationship with the surrounding landscape, and is the largest, and perhaps most creative, of all of Church's endeavors and it was, as he predicted, not completed during his lifetime.

[1] Professor David C. Huntington, author of *The Landscapes of Frederic Edwin Church, Vision of An American Era* (New York, 1966), was instrumental in the effort to preserve Olana as a historic site.

[2] This article is based upon a portion of my unpublished Ph.D. dissertation, "An Investigation of *Olana*, the Home of Frederic Edwin Church, Painter," Ohio University, 1973.

[3] The Studio Building, 15 Tenth Street, New York City, designed by Richard Morris Hunt in 1857, became an artists' center in New York. It contained studios of numerous painters, including Albert Bierstadt, Sanford R. Gifford, and Winslow Homer.

[4] Before his marriage Church had purchased a 126-acre working farm which constituted a part of his property at Olana (bill for architectural services, Richard Morris Hunt to Frederic Edwin Church, April 1861, in the Church archives, Olana).

[5] Letter from Frederic Edwin Church to William Henry Osborn, Rome, November 9, 1868, Church archives.

[6] Plans and elevations by Vaux, Withers and Company, Church archives.

[7] Letter from Frederic Edwin Church to William Henry Osborn, Rome, January 23, 1869, Church archives.

[8] Letter from Frederic Edwin Church to A. C. Goodman, Hudson, July 21, 1871, Church archives.

[9] The terms Oriental, meaning Eastern in a very broad sense, as well as Moorish and Muslim were often used in nineteenth-century sources and sometimes interchangeably.

[10] "In Summer Time on Olana," *Sunday Herald* (Boston), September 7, 1890.

[11] Ombra is the Italian word for shade, and it was used in the nineteenth century by Vaux and others to mean a shaded porch. The word appeared on the plans prepared by Vaux, Withers and Company.

[12] Letter from Frederic Edwin Church to Erastus Dow Palmer, Hudson, November 14, 1878, Palmer Papers, Albany Institute of History and Art.

[13] It has been suggested that Church was aided in his landscaping at Olana by Frederick Law Olmsted. However, to date, no written evidence has been found to support this assertion.

[14] At present visitors to Olana are not able to stop in cars near the front entrance, but must park in an unobtrusive parking lot north of the house.

[15] Letters from Frederic Edwin Church to Erastus Dow Palmer, Hudson, September 11, 1888, and April 19, 1891, Palmer Papers.

[16] A. J. Downing, *The Architecture of Country Houses* (New York, 1850; Dover reprint, New York, 1968), p. 263.

Mark Twain's house
in Hartford, Connecticut

BY WILSON H. FAUDE, *Curator, Mark Twain Memorial*

SAMUEL LANGHORNE CLEMENS, who wrote of the mighty Mississippi River under the pen name Mark Twain, spent his seventeen most productive years by the quiet, meandering Hog River in Hartford, Connecticut. The house which he built there at a cost of about $131,000 was completed in September 1874 at 351 Farmington Avenue and is now open to the public. A polychromatic, asymmetrical brownstone and brick structure with turrets and balconies, it was the only real home Clemens, his wife, and daughters Susy, Clara, and Jean ever knew.

Samuel Clemens first visited Hartford in 1868 to discuss with his friend Elisha Bliss, president of the American Publishing Company, the publication of *Innocents Abroad*. He wrote on that visit: "Of all the beautiful places it has been my fortune to see, this is the chief. You do not know what beauty is if you have not been here."[1] In 1870 Clemens married Olivia Langdon of Elmira, New York (Fig. 1). They lived for a short period in Buffalo and in 1871 moved to Hartford, then a literary and publishing center. In 1873 the Clemenses purchased land for their house on Farmington Avenue in an unfenced enclave known as Nook Farm. Charles Dudley Warner, an editor, essayist, and novelist, and the writer Harriet Beecher Stowe were their neighbors there. The informal atmosphere of Nook Farm, where children, parents, and guests were welcome in every house, provided Clemens with numerous friends and an ever-attentive audience.

According to Albert Bigelow Paine, Clemens found most contemporary Hartford houses "mainly of the good-box form of architecture, perfectly square, typifying the commercial pursuits of many of their owners. Potter [Edward T. Potter of New York] agreed to get away from this idea, and a radical and even frenzied departure was the result."[2] The house Potter designed for Clemens had nineteen rooms, eighteen fireplaces, and five baths. Its broad, sweeping wooden cornices and gables make it more European than American; in fact German building magazines of the period show examples of picturesque villas close in character to Potter's designs. The *Hartford Daily Times* of March 23, 1874, commented on the partially completed house: "The novelty displayed in the architecture of the building, the oddity of its internal arrangement, and the fame of its owner, will all conspire to make it a house of note for a long time to come." But like any new homeowner, Samuel Clemens was beset with problems:

I have been bullyragged all day by the builder, by his foreman, by the architect, by the tapestry devil who is to upholster the furniture, by the idiot who is putting down the carpets, by the scoundrel who is setting up the billiard-table (and has left the balls in New York), by the wildcat who is sodding the ground

Fig. 1.   Olivia Langdon at the time she married Samuel L. Clemens in 1870. *Black and white illustrations are from the Mark Twain Memorial.*

Pl. I.   The library was painted peacock blue and stenciled in gold by Associated Artists in 1881. Here Clemens read to his family from his manuscripts, Shakespeare, and the Brownings, and told his daughters stories about each of the objects on the mantel, beginning with the portrait of the cat on the right and ending with the impressionistic watercolor portrait on the left. *Except as noted, color photographs are by E. Irving Blomstrann.*

Fig. 2.   Clemens working in the bed bought in Venice in 1878. He lies at the foot so as to see the ornately carved headboard.

Fig. 3.   The front hall was decorated by Associated Artists in Venetian red with black stenciling. The woodwork was stenciled in silver to give the effect of mother-of-pearl inlay. The hanging lantern and circular seat are part of the original furnishings.

and finishing the driveway (after the sun went down), by a book *agent*, whose body is in the back yard and the coroner notified.[3]

The house was the pride of its owners for many years, and they continually found ways of embellishing it. They bought the great ceiling-high Scottish mantel in the library (Pl. I) in 1874 from Ayton Castle near Edinburgh. Four years later in Venice they purchased a richly carved double bed surmounted with *putti* (Fig. 2). In 1881 Samuel Clemens enlisted Louis C. Tiffany and Associated Artists (Samuel Colman, Lockwood de Forest, and Candace Wheeler) to redecorate the hall (Fig. 3) and the principal rooms on the ground floor (Pls. I, II). This important decorating firm, whose commissions included the redecoration of the White House in 1882, transformed the rooms from "awful Victorian" to "something much lighter"[4] which had a "suggestively divine quality."[5]

In this setting were written *The Adventures of Tom Sawyer, The Adventures of Huckleberry Finn, A Tramp Abroad, The Prince and the Pauper, Life on the Mississippi,* and *A Connecticut Yankee in King Arthur's Court.* To William Dean Howells and others, the house represented Clemens' "love of magnificence as if it had been another sealskin coat [see Fig. 4], and he was at the crest of the prosperity which enabled him to humor every whim or extravagance."[6] To the Clemenses it was home (Fig. 5). Here their daughters took their lessons or listened to their ever-indulgent father read aloud from his manuscripts or tell them stories. Here they dramatized for the family and neighbors scenes from Clemens' novel *The Prince and*

Fig. 4.   Clemens in his great sealskin coat.

Fig. 5.   The Clemens family on the porch of the Hartford house in 1885. They are, from left to right: Clara, Olivia, Jean, Samuel, and Susy. The dog's name was Hash.

Pl. II. Dining room. The table is one of the original furnishings, as is the silver epergne (see Fig. 7), which was on the Clemenses' wedding table. The wallpaper is an exact reproduction of the original embossed paper of rampant lilies installed by Associated Artists. The gold-stenciled woodwork is attributed to Samuel Colman of Associated Artists.

Pl. III. *Samuel Langhorne Clemens* (1835-1910), by James Carroll Beckwith (1852-1917), 1890. Beckwith, like Clemens, was a native of Hannibal, Missouri. Oil on canvas, 24 by 18 inches. *Mark Twain Memorial.*

Pl. IV.   The schoolroom was designed as a study for Clemens, but he found he could not work there because the view from the windows was too distracting, so it was turned over to his daughters for their lessons. He brought the fans above the piano back from the Hawaiian Islands for his daughters. Here the girls and their friends acted out the dramas written by neighbors about Queen Elizabeth and Mary, Queen of Scots, and held concerts at the J. and C. Fisher piano.

Pl. V.   The billiard room on the third floor became Clemens' study and retreat. In the pigeonholes to the right of the fireplace he deposited, and then forgot for months, everything from field glasses and boots to the unfinished manuscript of *The Adventures of Huckleberry Finn.* When he felt drained, he would play billiards. He justified this diversion from writing: ''When the tank runs dry you've only to leave it alone and it will fill up again in time'' (*Mark Twain in Eruption: Hitherto Unpublished Papers About Man and Events*, ed. Bernard De Voto, New York, 1940, p. 196).

Fig. 6. Susy Clemens and her friend Daisy Warner acting out a dramatization of Clemens' novel *The Prince and the Pauper*.

the Pauper (Fig. 6). Dinner parties were nightly events, for there was a continual flow of guests and visitors. Thomas Nast, Edwin Booth, Thomas Bailey Aldrich, William Dean Howells, generals Sheridan and Sherman, Sir Henry M. Stanley, Moncure Conway, Bret Harte, and Rudyard Kipling were among those who journeyed to Hartford and spent hours, days, or even weeks in the house. Many complained of the late hours, the quantities of liquor consumed, and the exhausting conversations which left them like "empty locust shells,"[7] but an invitation to return was never refused. A brass plaque just above the library fireplace summed up the warm hospitality characteristic of the house: *The ornament of a house is the friends who frequent it.*

Because of unwise investments and the ever-increasing cost of his lavish standard of living, Samuel Clemens closed his Hartford house in 1891 and began to make extended lecture tours in this country and abroad in order to replenish his finances. In August 1896, as she was to sail to Europe to join her parents, Susy, Clemens' eldest and favorite daughter, became ill. The house was reopened, but before her mother could reach America to take care of her, Susy died in the mahogany guest room. She was twenty-four. Mrs. Clemens would never cross the threshold of the house again, while to Clemens it became a holy place, a shrine. He could never conquer the feeling that if his unwise

investments had not made paupers of them all, Susy would not have died.

The house was sold in 1903 to the president of a fire-insurance company. From then until 1929, it served successively as a residence, a private school for boys, a warehouse, and an apartment building. In 1929 it was purchased as a memorial to Mark Twain at the inflated price of $155,000. Because of a heavy mortgage and high maintenance costs, it was impossible to think of restoration for many years. In 1955 the trustees voted to restore the house to its original appearance, and in 1963 work began.

The restoration has been guided by one philosophy: that the house is a document and the trustees could only return it to the original text. This emphasis on accuracy has involved checking all manuscripts that might refer to the house, a room, or an object. Contemporaries of the Clemens daughters who remembered the house as children were interviewed. Most important of all has been meticulous investigation of the house itself. The painstaking removal of layers of paint has revealed fragments of the original wall colors and designs. Tack holes in the floor revealed the original width, weight, and even type of carpets. No object, piece of furniture, or decorative motif not clearly substantiated by research was permitted in the restoration.

From the beginning, those involved in the restoration sensibly realized that if it were to be done, Hartford must do it. The house is supported by memberships and donations; local foundations and the state have provided some matching grants; the Garden Club of Hartford gave money to restore the grounds; volunteers have researched the documents, located original and period objects, and conducted the membership and fund-raising drives. It has been a long and demanding task, but a rewarding one, for the result is Samuel Clemens' house, a century old this autumn, restored as accurately as possible to its former grandeur— the beloved house which Mark Twain eulogized:

To us, our house was not unsentient matter—it had a heart, and a soul, and eyes to see us with; and approvals and solicitudes, and deep sympathies; it was of us, and we were in its confidence, and lived in its grace and in the peace of its benediction. We 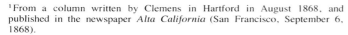 up and speak out its eloquent welcome—and we could not enter it unmoved.[8]

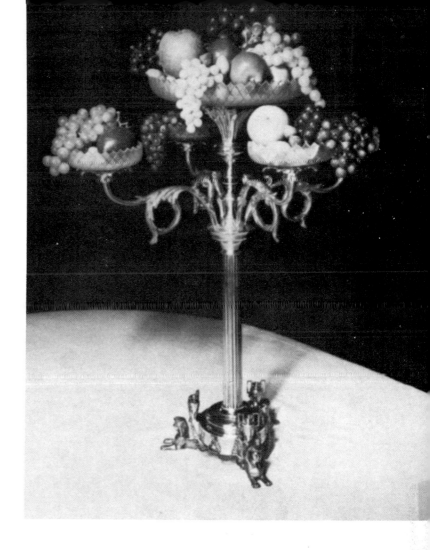

Fig. 7. Silver epergne that was on the table during the wedding of Samuel Clemens and Olivia Langdon.

[1] From a column written by Clemens in Hartford in August 1868, and published in the newspaper *Alta California* (San Francisco, September 6, 1868).

[2] Albert Bigelow Paine, *Mark Twain, a Biography* (New York, 1912), Vol. 1, p. 480.

[3] *Ibid.*, p. 520.

[4] Letter from Harriet Foote Taylor to Edith C. Salsbury, Little Compton, Rhode Island, May 3, 1959, now in the Mark Twain Memorial Collection.

[5] Letter from Clara Clemens Samossoud to Robert H. Schutz, San Diego, California, February 21, 1959, now in the Mark Twain Memorial Collection.

[6] William Dean Howells, *My Mark Twain* (New York, 1910), p. 7.

[7] *Ibid.*, p. 9.

[8] *Mark Twain's Letters*, comp. Albert Bigelow Paine (New York), 1917, Vol. 2, p. 641.

Fig. 8. Susy Clemens' christening cup, made by Tiffany and Company. It is inscribed on one side *Olivia Susan Clemens,/March 19th 1872*, and on the other *from Grandma* (Mrs. Jervis Langdon).

The Magoffin homestead, an adobe in El Paso

BY BETSY KNIGHT

Fig. 1. *Military Post, El Paso, Texas*, by John Russell Bartlett, 1850-1851. Sepia watercolor, 8⅛ by 11⅜ inches. The bleak quality of frontier life and the ruggedness of the region are clearly evident in this view of Smith's Ranch, about two miles up the Rio Grande from the original Magoffin house. *John Carter Brown Library, Providence.*

ALMOST UNKNOWN to East Texas for much of the nineteenth century, El Paso del Norte, a Spanish town across the Rio Grande from the present city of El Paso, was settled in the 1860's. No fixed routes crossed the Texas no-man's land from east to west, and El Paso del Norte became known only to traders and travelers along the Santa Fe Trail, which stretched from Independence, Missouri, to Chihuahua and Durango in northern Mexico.

James Wiley Magoffin (Pl. II), a Kentuckian of Irish descent, was for twenty years a trader on the trail, an occupation which brought him a sizable fortune.[1] He served as American consul in Saltillo, where his wit, good nature, and lavish hospitality earned him the title "Don Santiago." While in Mexico he married Doña Maria Gertrudis Valdez de Beremende, whose cousin Manuel Armijo later became governor of the Mexican province of New Mexico.[2]

In 1846 President James Knox Polk instructed General Stephen Watts Kearny to engage Magoffin to pave the way for the peaceful occupation of New Mexico during the Mexican War. This Magoffin was able to do through his connection with Governor Armijo, and Kearny entered Santa Fe without encountering any resistance.[3]

Later Magoffin was called upon to arrange the peaceful takeover of the province of Chihuahua by General J. E. Wool. However, the Mexicans arrested the trader near El Paso del Norte (now Juarez) and imprisoned him for nine months. It appears, however, that Magoffin led a charmed life. When another trader was arrested carrying a letter to Magoffin from General Kearny praising him for his help in taking New Mexico—a certain death warrant if it had been read—the Mexican officer in charge gave it to Magoffin unopened, suggesting that he burn it if it was

Pl. 1. Thick adobe walls form a natural vestibule for the double doorway giving onto the patio of the Magoffin house. The pediment is plainer than those above the door and windows on the north façade (see Pl. IV). The delicately painted geometric and leaf patterns on the lower panels are reminiscent of the motifs used by Charles Locke Eastlake. *Except as noted, photographs are by Helga Photo Studio.*

Fig. 2. North, or entrance, façade of the Magoffin house in a photograph taken before 1900 (see also Pl. IV).

not important. Magoffin is reported to have said that it took 2,900 bottles of champagne to obtain his freedom, and he eventually received $30,000 from the United States government for services rendered.[4]

After his release from prison in 1847 Magoffin became the first settler of what is now El Paso, on the American side of the Rio Grande opposite El Paso del Norte. There in 1849 he built a large adobe house and ranch buildings around a plaza. The settlement became known as Magoffinsville.[5] Magoffin's house, because of its size and the hospitable nature of its owner, became an attraction for visitors to the region. In the fall of 1850 John Russell Bartlett (Pl. III) established the headquarters of the United States Boundary Commission in the house and in February 1851 gave a dinner there for the Mexican commission followed by a ball and supper attended by about fifty ladies. Of the occasion Bartlett later wrote:

Mr. Magoffin, whose house, in which I had my quarters, was the most spacious on the river, threw the whole open for the occasion, giving me thereby ample accommodations for the large party which had assembled. But as the greater portion of the company lived on the opposite bank of the river, it was no easy matter to get them together. I therefore sent my carriage, and others that were kindly furnished me, for my guests; and as it was between three and four miles from my quarters to El Paso, including the fording of the Rio Grande, it was necessary to begin fetching them at the unfashionable hour of four o'clock in the afternoon. The river had to be forded by daylight, in consequence of the frequent changes in the channel and the bars.

Fig. 3. Joseph Magoffin (1837-1923), colored photograph, 29 by 24 inches. Joseph, the son of James Wiley Magoffin, built the present house. He was born in Chihuahua, Mexico, and was educated in Lexington, Kentucky, and St. Louis. In 1856 he joined his father in the mercantile business in El Paso. After the Civil War Joseph was mayor of El Paso for four terms as well as county commissioner, county judge, justice of the peace, and customs collector. During his lifetime he was generally considered the first citizen of El Paso. *Private collection.*

Fig. 4. Settee; height 48, length 66 inches. The fretwork of the
arms and the incised carving on this settee and the four matching
armchairs (see Pl. V) are typical of Eastlake decoration. However,
the remarkable cresting rails make it tempting to believe that the
set was made locally. Flanking a horseshoe that is complete with
nail holes and toe and heel calks are Mexican eagles easily distin-
guished by their characteristic crest.

Pl. II. *James Wiley Magoffin* (1799-1868), by Henry Cheever Pratt (1803-1880), 1852. Oil on canvas, 35½ by 28½ inches. This portrait was painted while Pratt was a member of John Russell Bartlett's United States Boundary Commission. The patio and *corredor* in the background probably do not resemble those at Magoffin's house. They do, however, reflect the impression all visitors received of Magoffin as one of the most important proprietors in the Southwest. *Private collection.*

I was quite at a loss for furniture and fittings for my entertainment. Chairs were borrowed of the neighbors far and near; but even with these I had not half seats enough for the company. This, however, proved no great inconvenience; for the Mexican ladies, preferring to sit *á la Turk*, formed a double row around the dancing room. The señoras occupied the trunks, chairs, and settees, and the señoritas the carpet in front. . . . To light the large hall properly most tried my ingenuity; but this difficulty was overcome by means of a new-fashioned chandelier improvised by one of our gentlemen for the occasion. Sockets for the candles were first required; and these were constructed out of the tin boxes in which sardines had been preserved. Next, a hoop from a pork barrel was divested of its bark, and wrapped around with binding of a bright scarlet hue, which had been brought out to decorate the heads of the fair Apaches and Comanches, as well as the tails and manes of their animals. Into this hoop or frame the tin sockets were fixed, and the whole supported by several loops of the same elegant material fastened to a common centre. Such was the style and origin of our chandeliers, with their dozen burners each; four of which, suspended from the ceiling, shed such a ray of light upon the festal hall, as rendered the charms of the fair señoritas doubly captivating. The evening passed off pleasantly; and all danger of crossing the river was obviated by the company remaining til eight o'clock the following morning.[6]

Bartlett left El Paso for Washington in October 1852 after a dinner given for him by Magoffin which featured

what Bartlett called "a cold collation which could have done credit to the caterer of a metropolitan hotel. Although it is difficult at times to procure a piece of fresh meat at El Paso, the delicacies prepared in New York and Paris for foreign markets can always be found here in abundance though at high cost."[7] A year later another visitor found Magoffin "living quite in nabob style in a large Spanish-built house that reminded me somewhat of an old mansion of the feudal ages."[8]

Because James Magoffin sided with the Confederacy during the Civil War, his property was confiscated and half of it was sold at auction in 1865. The house, which had been sold, was washed away when the Rio Grande flooded in 1868. Magoffin died later that year, and it was not until 1873 that his son Joseph (Fig. 3) managed to recover the portion of the property which had not been sold.

We know only that the original house was built of adobe. In all probability the floors were of dirt packed almost as hard as stone. Canvas was often nailed over these dirt floors and carpets laid on the canvas.[9]

Joseph Magoffin built the present homestead in 1875 as a replica of the one that was washed away, according to family tradition. Today it is ten blocks from the center of downtown El Paso, but in 1877 it was described as a "magnificent country seat."[10] The present house is a one-story, U-shape building around a central patio. It is built of adobe brick made of sun-baked mud and straw,

Pl. III. *John Russell Bartlett* (1805-1886), by Leola Freeman. Oil on canvas, 33½ by 27½ inches. This is a copy of the portrait by Pratt now in the Amon Carter Museum of Western Art in Fort Worth. Through the window can be seen the crumbling clay banks of the Rio Grande, which formed much of the United States boundary with Mexico. Magoffin's house, where Bartlett was quartered, was in fact half a mile from the center of the channel. *Private collection.*

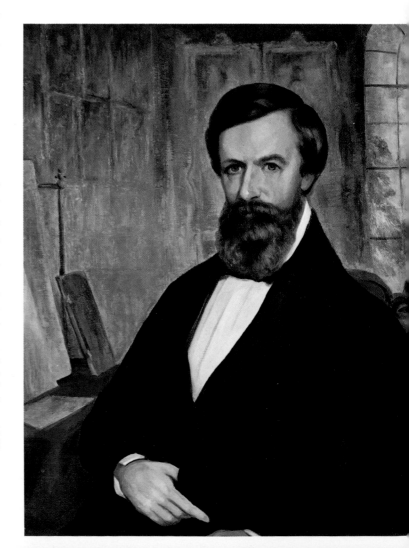

and its walls are three to four feet thick. Most of the ceilings and floors are made of pine matchboard. The fourteen-foot-ceilings, covered by a one-foot layer of adobe for insulation, are supported by roughly-finished pine rafters, or vigas. No nails were used in any part of the original construction.

The lumber for the house was brought from the Sacramento Mountains in New Mexico, some eighty miles away, which was the closest source of large timbers. All the principal rooms have adobe fireplaces, some with mantelpieces which were added later. Wall niches and built-in cabinets, wrought-iron chandeliers, and occasional decorative tiles set into the walls give a Mexican feeling to the interior.

The double doors at each end of the central hall (Pl. V) have colored-glass side lights and transoms, a treatment that is probably a faithful copy of that in the original house. A portrait that Henry Cheever Pratt painted of Bartlett in the house in 1852 (of which a copy is shown in Pl. III) shows a window with colored-glass panes in the background. The ample hall of the present house conforms in spirit to the Spanish-Mexican *zaguán*, an open passageway leading through a house to the patio. Today the hall is used as a parlor just as the *zaguán* was always the center of activity.

Pl. IV. The 103-foot north façade of the Magoffin house (see also Fig. 2). In the late nineteenth century the walls of the wing were rusticated, but their original smooth finish has been restored by the application of many coats of adobe, the last of which have been mixed with waterproof plaster. Metal *canales*, or downspouts, drain the flat roof, which is ringed by a two-foot-high parapet.

Since the contents of the original house were washed away in 1868, the majority of the furniture dates from the 1870's and 1880's. Most of it was brought by wagon eleven hundred miles from St. Louis or, after a sea journey, seven hundred miles overland from Port Lavaca on the Texas coast. A few pieces may be of local origin. Andrew Hornick, a Bavarian cabinetmaker, is known to have worked in El Paso from 1854 until 1899.

Joseph Magoffin served four terms as mayor of El Paso and was one of its leading citizens. His home, like his father's, continued to be the center of the city's social life.

Magoffin's daughter Josephine married General William Jefferson Glasgow. He was the son of Edward James Glasgow of St. Louis, who had been United States consul at Guaymas, Mexico, before he was twenty years old, and who later was a trader on the Santa Fe Trail. Their daughter, Octavia Magoffin Glasgow, lives in the house today.

[1] James Magoffin's brothers Samuel and William were also Santa Fe Trail traders. Another brother, Beriah, was governor of Kentucky from 1859 to 1862.

[2] She was also the niece of Juan Martin de Veramendi, whose daughter Ursula married Jim Bowie in 1831. Veramendi was governor of Texas-Coahuila from November 1832 until his death in February 1833.

[3] Thomas Hart Benton, *Thirty Years View* (New York, 1856), Vol. 2, pp. 682-684. Benton, who suggested Magoffin to President Polk, gives a complete account of Magoffin's role in the affair.

[4] Benton, *Thirty Years View*, pp. 682-684, says that Magoffin paid $50 for each dozen bottles of champagne, but it is doubtful that a $12,000 claim for this purpose would have been allowed by the government, and Magoffin's $30,000 compensation must have been for other expenses.

[5] The present city of El Paso grew up around Franklin, a small settlement a mile or so from Magoffinsville. In 1854 the military post for the region was established at Magoffinsville and named Fort Bliss.

[6] John R. Bartlett, *Personal Narrative of Explorations and Incidents in Texas...*, (New York, 1854), Vol. 1, pp. 167-168.

[7] *Ibid.*, Vol. 2, p. 402.

[8] W. W. H. Davis, *El Gringo: or New Mexico and her People* (New York, 1857), p. 376.

[9] Lydia Spencer Lane, *I Married a Soldier* (Philadelphia, 1893), p. 68. Mrs. Lane accompanied her husband to Fort Bliss, then at Magoffinsville, in 1859.

[10] C. L. Sonnichsen, *Pass of the North* (El Paso, 1968), p. 211.

Fig. 5.   The recessed shelves and free-form curves within the pediment of this cupboard are typical Mexican-Spanish details.

Fig. 6. Cabinet, 1890-1900. The rocker of about the same time may be a locally made piece incorporating Eastlake designs. The yokelike leather-covered cresting rail, exaggerated rope turnings, and wagon-wheel detail of the back seem Western motifs, while the nail studding around the leather seat and back is a Mexican detail.

Pl. V. The *zaguán*, or central hall, which serves as a parlor, is fifteen feet wide by thirty-two feet long. It easily accommodates the piano made by W. H. Knabe and Sons of Baltimore, which was most likely brought by sea to Texas and then overland to El Paso.

Above the piano is a large Mexican painting of the Virgin, probably of the early eighteenth century. The portrait at the right of the fireplace is of Brigadier General William Jefferson Glasgow, the father of the present owner.

Pl. VI. This bed, just short of thirteen feet tall, is part of a set that comprises a mirrored wardrobe and a marble-topped chest with full-length pier glass. The suite is said to have come from New Orleans. Burl-veneer panels adorn head and foot boards. The tufting in the canopy is original. The flat carving on the small chair in the foreground may possibly indicate a Mexican origin.

The Open Gates:
the George Sealy house in Galveston

BY ELEANOR H. GUSTAFSON

WHEN GEORGE SEALY SR., a prominent banker and businessman in Galveston, decided to build The Open Gates in 1881, he purchased property at Broadway and Twenty-fifth Street there from the widow of E. B. Nichols, who had been a Confederate general during the Civil War. Later he is said to have sent his wife, Magnolia, to New York City to hire "the finest Architect in the country." Whether or not this is the case, the design of the house has long been attributed to Stanford White, of the firm of McKim, Mead and White, although no plan for it has been located. However, there does exist a typed manuscript of specifications for the interior of the house (see p. 109) prepared by McKim, Mead and White in October 1888. If White was in fact the architect, the Sealy house is the only known building in the South designed by him.

According to an unpublished history of the house written in 1953 by the first owner's daughter Margaret Sealy Burton, McKim, Mead and White arranged to send to Galveston "bricks, tiles, and white stone decorations of carved and moulded festoons of fruit and flowers [which]

The Open Gates, the George Sealy house in Galveston. "When my mother returned with the plans, my father had purchased . . . the whole block occupied by General E. B. Nichols. . . . In front of this lovely home [General Nichols'] rose an enormous pine tree. . . . At the back and west end of the grounds they had built long barracks for the cavalry. . . . General Nichols home, barracks, and the pine tree were demolished to make room for our new house and the winding driveway. . . . It took at least a year and a half to complete the house and landscape the grounds."

Entrance to the George Sealy house. During the great hurricane of 1900 "as people were swept in the turbulent waters they were pulled into the boats by the sailors who had their boats tied to our fence, and a large number of people were saved by others who were standing on our porch upstairs. They grabbed them by the hair or any place they could hold to and pulled them up to the porch. We opened our doors to the unfortunates. The house was filled all day and night with over 400 people who came there for safety, or had been rescued from a watery grave. The windows of the basement had been smashed with floating debris. For weeks there was 15 ft. of sea water there which reached to the beautifully polished oak floors above." *Photograph by Helga Photo Studio.*

had been shipped to New York from foreign countries," the bricks from England, and the rounded terra-cotta roof tiles from Belgium. Tiles left over after the roof was completed were used to edge the magnificent gardens, but many of these now replace roof tiles that have been destroyed during the house's eighty-six-year history.

The house had the first cellar in Galveston and in the attic is a large room with a stage that was used for family entertainments. Except for the solarium, which is located

Central hall, looking north toward the polygonal stair hall (top), and south toward the front door (bottom). Over the door leading to the library in the bottom picture is a portrait of George Sealy Sr., the builder of the house. "We had an old moose head over the mantle piece in the hall. My brother, George, bought it in Canada, where he went hunting one fall. This old moose was stuffed with some sort of glue. It melted all summer and ran down his nose so badly in streams that we always had to keep a tin bucket underneath to catch the water. He cried all summer, but in the winter he froze up and never shed a drop."

"The dining room was Honduras mahogany. The huge dining table and buffet were made especially to fit in the room. The buffet had a leaded glass pane china cabinet overhead. All the walls and ceiling beams and wainscoting were of mahogany. The sides of the room were of red canvas studded with designs in brass nails. The light fixtures were of Sheffield silver."

in the tower at the southeast corner, the major rooms on the first floor surround a central hall. To the south is the library; to the west is the drawing room, one end of which is a "music room" with a concave ceiling; and to the east are the dining room, pantry, and kitchen. The four second-floor bedrooms are also arranged around a central hall, the spaces generally corresponding to those below. While the house was sumptuously furnished from the start, many of the unusual furnishings were purchased many years later, during Mrs. Sealy's frequent trips to Europe after her husband died in 1901. In 1915 Mrs. Sealy had Elsie de Wolfe redecorate the house with new draperies, rugs, and upholstery, and in a few instances new furniture.

In October 1969 the house was listed on the National Register of Historic Places, and in the same month the builder's son Robert Sealy, in the name of surviving members of the family and heirs, deeded The Open Gates complete with its original furnishings to the Board of Regents of the University of Texas System. Mr. Sealy maintains life tenancy in the house, which will eventually be used by the University's John Sealy Hospital as a hospitality house and faculty club. As such it will stand as a perpetual memorial to George and Magnolia Sealy and to the elegance of early Galveston.

Library, as redecorated by Elsie de Wolfe in 1915.

Two views of the drawing room. The ceiling is covered with canvas which was originally painted sky blue. ''The large parlor had yellow brocade satin covering the walls. The woodwork was white and gilt.''

Upstairs bedroom. "The gorgeous hand painted bedroom set in mother's room is distinctly French, it being painted in festoons of pink roses, green leaves and garlands, also turquoise ribbons all on tan satin wood like the museum pieces painted years ago by a famous artist named Verni Martin."

SPECIFICATIONS
of

Work to be done and material furnished for the completion of a part of the first floor and second story hall of a dwelling house for GEORGE SEALY, ESQ., Galveston, Texas, in accordance with the drawings and specifications prepared by and under the general superintendence of

McKIM, MEAD AND WHITE,
Architects,
57 Broadway, New York City

October 1888.

JOINERY.

WORKMANSHIP:

The workmanship is to be thorough and equal to the best in every respect.

MATERIALS:

All the materials required, herein described, or specified are to be of the best, and the woods are to be absolutely clear and free from knots, cracks, sap, or other defects.

All to be thoroughly seasoned and kiln dried, and protected from the weather after leaving the kiln until in place in the house and the work accepted, and to be warranted to stand for one year without opening at joints, warping or cracking.

Wherever wide panels, or other wide plain surfaces are used in base-boards or other wall surfaces, the wood is to be put together with neatly matched grain and dovetailed cleats on the back side in such a manner as to allow the wood to expand or contract, is not to be nailed on more than one side, and is to be dowelled to other standing finish where possible.

Between the upper and under floors throughout two layers of resin sized sheathing felt are to be laid.

All panel work is to be full framed work, made and fitted at the shops, as far as possible, and all to receive a coat of paint on the back before it leaves the shop.

Full sized detail drawings, in addition to the scale drawings, will be furnished for all moulded, cut or carved work, and are to be accurately followed.

All the standing finish, including doors, is to be hand-smoothed before being set in place.

All the work, after being set in place, is to be protected from injury by other workmen and the floors especially are to be covered with thick sheathing felt as soon as laid, and to be kept thus protected until all painters and other workmen are out of the building, and then to be thoroughly scraped and smoothed down and left absolutely perfect when the house is completed.

To be put up complete in the house and to include the entire finish of front doors, vestibule doors, first story hall, main staircase, second story hall, drawing room, music room, library and dining room, and to include the finish of all cabinet work, hardware, facings and hearths for fireplaces, registers, painting of walls or covering with stuffs, and painting and decoration of ceilings.

The front doors 4 inches thick, veneered both sides with American oak, with single panel with carved disk in the middle.

Vestibule to have plain mosaic floor at one dollar ($1.00) a foot; wainscot and ceiling of simple oak panelling. The glass panel in door and side lights at two dollars ($2.00) per foot. The hardware of dark bronze finish.

Hall floor in American oak, in squares with plain border. Hearth and facings of speckled gold brick. Woodwork and ceiling beams throughout of American quartered oak, as shown.

Staircase of American oak, as shown, all panellings carried up to wainscot in second story hall.

Finish of second story hall, floor in squares or narrow strips; panelled wainscot, door and door trim and moulded cornice one foot high, all of American oak. Windows on staircase in stained glass at three dollars ($3.00) a foot. The hardware and metal throughout this hall work to be of bronze.

Drawing room and music room in enamelled white and gold finish, as shown; walls covered with yellow silk and ceiling painted in imitation of sky; gold hardware throughout; facings and hearth in Algerian onyx.

Finish of library in cherry, with book-cases, as shown, with glass doors and wood muntins; floor in cherry; a plain plastered ceiling, decorated in simple colors; tapestry panels in walls; hardware in copper; Numidian marble for hearth and facings.

Dining room with wainscot, as shown, with mahogany glued up with wainscot in one piece; ceiling mahogany with boxed beams and plain painted panels between; fireplace with Sienna marble facings; walls covered with fibrine; floor of oak.

Two views of an upstairs bedroom. "The next bedroom furnishings came from Italy. It [the bed] was beautifully carved in dark oak, ornamented with cupids on the head and foot posts. There were chairs, tables, and a day couch to match. The china Della Robia ornaments were blue and white pottery medallions with bambinos. They were hung around the borders of the ceiling and tall vases on the mantle. A large carved oak chest held the blankets and bed linen."

Biltmore in Asheville, North Carolina

BY SUSANNE BRENDEL-PANDICH, *Curator*

WHILE MOST members of the Vanderbilt family were building mansions on Fifth Avenue in New York and in Newport, Rhode Island, George Washington Vanderbilt (Fig. 1) was planning the construction of Biltmore, a self-sufficient estate of approximately 125,000 acres in Asheville in the Appalachian Mountains of western North Carolina. George Vanderbilt was the youngest of William H. Vanderbilt's eight children and the grandson of Commodore Cornelius Vanderbilt. His sensitive nature had led his parents to believe that he would take up the ministry but, while

Pl. I. Main, or eastern, façade of Biltmore, designed by Richard Morris Hunt (see Pl. XI) and built for George W. Vanderbilt (see Fig. 1) between 1889 and 1895 in Asheville, North Carolina. The reflecting pool is part of the four-acre esplanade in front of the house, which is set at the end of an *allée* of poplars. *Photograph by Michael Kent Smith.*

Pl. II. A pergola overgrown with wisteria forms one side of the terrace at the southern end of the house. It is on one of a series of terraces on many levels designed by Frederick Law Olmsted (see Fig. 8). *Smith photograph.*

he remained a strongly religious man, he chose to pursue art, literature, and science with the same determination with which most Vanderbilts pursued finance.

Based on European precedents, Biltmore was planned to incorporate a model farm and to be a center for the study of forestry, horticulture, and scientific farming. On February 20, 1897, two years after Biltmore was completed, the *Asheville News and Hotel Reporter* commented:

It is Vanderbilt the farmer, not Vanderbilt of the Chateau, who has proven to be the great benefactor of Western North Carolina. He has shown the Carolinians the productive capacities of their virgin soil . . . by the scientific drainage, the improved machinery, the importation of fine stock, the judicious and lavish use of fertilizers, and the most up-to-date and scientific methods of farming.[1]

Vanderbilt started planning his estate shortly after his father's death in 1885. He had inherited the Homestead, the family's farm on Staten Island, and

Pl. III. The western façade of Biltmore is mirrored in one of a series of watercourses that Olmsted placed along the carriage drives on the estate. *Smith photograph.*

made many improvements to it,[2] but it was a small farm and could not be developed along the lines Vanderbilt envisioned.

It is possible that Vanderbilt's delicate health first brought him to Asheville, whose mountain air was thought to be therapeutic. The town had a number of elegant resort hotels in the late nineteenth century and was a prestigious center for the treatment of tuberculosis.

Apparently, Vanderbilt came upon the site of Biltmore while strolling through the woods and found the view so beautiful that he bought the farm on which he stood. He continued to buy surrounding farms until he had acquired 125,000 acres, including Mount Pisgah, the highest peak on the horizon,[3] To guide him in his project Vanderbilt engaged Richard Morris Hunt as his architect and Frederick Law Olmsted as his landscape architect. The three men exchanged ideas freely on all aspects of the planning of Biltmore.

By the late 1880's Hunt's practice was thriving, and among his prestigious clients were Astors, Vanderbilts, Belmonts, Delanos, and Gerrys. In addition to the palatial residences he built for these families, Hunt designed such public structures as the administration building at the World's Columbian Exposition of 1893 in Chicago, the Lenox Library in New York City, the base of the Statue of Liberty, and the Fogg Museum of Harvard University.

He was affiliated with the Vanderbilt family from 1878 until his death in 1895. The magnificent French château he completed for William K. Vanderbilt in 1881 at 660 Fifth Avenue was a milestone for both the family and the architect. Despite their wealth, the Vanderbilts had been excluded from New York society and had never been invited to the Patriarch's Ball, at which what were known as the four hundred gathered each season.[4] William K. Vanderbilt opened his

Fig. 1. George Washington Vanderbilt (1862–1914), in a photograph of 1914. The builder of Biltmore was the youngest child of William H. Vanderbilt and the grandson of Commodore Cornelius Vanderbilt.

Fig. 2. Front, or eastern, elevation of Biltmore. This is one of nine hundred architectural drawings of the house that are now in the archives of Biltmore. Hunt assigned a full-time supervising architect and two draftsmen to the site as well as forwarding detailed drawings from his New York office. *Photograph by William A. V. Cecil.*

Fig. 3. Rendering of the western façade of Biltmore by Hunt, c. 1889. Watercolor on paper, 16 by 33½ inches. Not shown are the stables that were built at the north end of the house and the large terrace built at the south end. Those additions were suggested by Olmsted, the landscape architect of Biltmore. *Cecil photograph.*

Pl. IV. This huge wrought-iron chandelier is suspended at the center of the four-story grand staircase. *Photograph by Alderman Studios.*

new house with a magnificent ball, and shortly thereafter the Vanderbilts were invited to their first Patriarch's Ball. Hunt also designed the Vanderbilt mausoleum (1881–1889) on Staten Island; Marble House (1888–1892) and the Breakers (1892–1895), both in Newport; and Biltmore (1889–1895).

Biltmore was the last and the largest of his commissions, and Hunt was especially attached to the project since he and his client got on splendidly and even made several trips to Europe together to collect ideas and furnishings for the house. Hunt's wife wrote in her diary in 1894, "[Richard] always went to Biltmore full in [*sic*] anticipation of pleasure, for here George Vanderbilt watched over him with affectionate solicitude. . . . even his professional work was made easy by the perfect harmony between himself and his client."[5]

Frederick Olmsted also had a close working relationship with Vanderbilt. The Olmsteds had been neighbors of the Vanderbilts on Staten Island, and Frederick Olmsted had worked on the Vanderbilt mausoleum in the 1880's and on George Vanderbilt's Bar Harbor estate, Pointe D'Acadie, in the early 1890's. When he took on Biltmore, his last great commission, he had already established himself as one of America's foremost and most prolific landscape architects, having designed parks in New York, Boston, and a score of smaller cities.

Olmsted's many letters about the project reveal his zeal. He helped Vanderbilt bring together some of the greatest names in horticulture and dendrology in America. Gifford Pinchot (1865–1946), who later became the first head of the Bureau of Forestry under Theodore Roosevelt, was made consulting forester.

Pl. V. The ceiling of the enormous banquet hall arches seventy feet above the seventy-two- by forty-two-foot floor. The room was designed around the sixteenth-century Brussels tapestries depicting Venus and Vulcan which Vanderbilt bought at the Hôtel Drouot in Paris on May 23, 1887. The oak dining table and the canopied chair against the wall were designed by Hunt. The large set of walnut arm and side chairs dates from the nineteenth century. *Alderman Studios photograph.*

Charles S. Sargent (1841–1927), one of America's leading nineteenth-century horticulturists, was also an advisor at Biltmore. Indeed, the first American experiments in practical forestry took place on the estate.[6]

Olmsted sent his son Frederick Law Olmsted Jr., known as Rick, to Biltmore to observe the unique work taking place. He reminded him by letter, "Keep clearly in mind that which is the main essential object of this Biltmore school; gaining such knowledge of plants as you get in no other. . . . If Mr. Vanderbilt were putting all his wealth at your disposal, you could not be better situated than you are with reference to education."[7]

Olmsted also contributed to the design of the house by suggesting that the stables be grouped at the north end and a terrace be built out from the south end.[8] These were obviously additions to the original plan, for they do not appear on an early rendering of the house by Hunt (Fig. 3).

Hunt and Olmsted had collaborated amicably on projects in the past and, as Olmsted wrote,

Here again, at Biltmore we have managed to reconcile the requirements of Hunt, in his Renaissance Buildings with a generally picturesque natural character in the approaches, and in the main landscape features; introducing more or less formal . . . outworks of architectural motive for that purpose. . . . There has not been the slightest lack

Fig. 4. Main entrance to Biltmore in a photograph of c. 1895. The staircase tower is modeled on that at the château of Blois in France. Vanderbilt had Thomas H. Lindsey, an Asheville photographer, record the construction of the house and the progress of the landscaping (see also Figs. 5-7).

Fig. 5. Billiard room and carriage porch under construction on the south end of the house, in a photograph taken on November 24, 1893.

Pl. VI. The breakfast room, or family dining room, is hung with Vanderbilt family portraits. The walls are covered with stamped Spanish leather. The jasperware fireplace surround is eighteenth-century Wedgwood. The table and chairs date from the nineteenth century. *Alderman Studios photograph.*

of harmony between us. He has accepted every single suggestion that I have made and I have accepted every single suggestion that he has made and I do not think there will be a note of discord in the combined work.[9]

Like the castles of the Loire valley, Biltmore is situated among the rolling Carolina mountains with the French Broad River gently winding through the bottom land. Its exterior (Pls. I, II, and III) incorporates all the elements of an early sixteenth-century French château, to which it is comparable in scale, with a façade 780 feet long and a floor area of four acres. The vertical Gothic elements are emphasized by the tall, narrow windows and the high pitched roof. Gargoyles, pinnacles, and chimneys erupt from

Pl. VII. The library contains more than twenty thousand volumes, for Vanderbilt was a bibliophile. The wooden figures of Demeter, goddess of the earth, and Hestia, goddess of the hearth, flanking the overmantel were carved by Karl Bitter (1867-1915), who also cast the iron andirons representing Vulcan and Venus. His work appears throughout Biltmore, which was his largest residential commission. The ceiling painting depicting Aurora is attributed to Giovanni Antonio Pellegrini (1675-1741), and nineteenth-century records in the house confirm that the seventy-two- by thirty-foot canvas was shipped to Biltmore from Joseph Spiridon of Paris in 1895. *Alderman Studios photograph.*

Fig. 6. Construction of the second floor under way, in a photograph of c. 1893. Beneath the limestone facing is a brick core bound together by metal I-beams.

Fig. 7. First stages of work on Biltmore village, outside the entrance to the estate, in a photograph of 1890–1895. All Souls Episcopal Church (Pl. X) is being built at the left. Between 1895 and 1900 the workers' houses in the foreground were replaced by half-timbered cottages. The source of the smoke in the background is the Asheville Tile and Woodworking Company, which was owned and operated by Vanderbilt for the construction of the estate.

Pl. VIII. Mrs. William H. Vanderbilt, the builder's mother, used the north bedroom. It is decorated in the Louis XV style, which was considered appropriate for a lady's room in the late nineteenth century. *Alderman Studios photograph.*

every corner. In the tympanums over the windows and in the copper work on the roof the architect recorded his patron forever by incorporating GV and the acorns of the Vanderbilt coat of arms. Renaissance elements of French sixteenth-century architecture are evident in the basic symmetry of the façade and the use of arched loggias and columns. Rick Olmsted wrote perceptively of Hunt's design in February 1895:

Whether we think with some that it and the whole Estate are un-American and out of accord with our nineteenth century feeling and civilization, or whether we think with others that this marks the beginning of an era of great American country places and country houses, we must at least accept it as a great Work of Art. So able and cool a critic as McKim ranks it with the very best work of the century throughout the world, and considers Mr. Hunt to have bettered his instructors of the Early French Renaissance. At all events it stands as the best work ever done by the leading architect of the country.[10]

Pl. IX. The south bedroom was Vanderbilt's, and is hung with prints, which he collected avidly. The walnut woodwork and massive Spanish, Portuguese, and Italian furniture have the appropriate dignity for the bedroom of the master of the house. *Alderman Studios photograph.*

Fig. 8. *Frederick Law Olmsted* (1822–1903), by John Singer Sargent (1856–1925), 1895. Signed and dated at lower right, *John S. Sargent 1895*. Oil on canvas, approximately 92 by 62 inches. The landscape architect is surrounded by North Carolina laurel, rhododendron, and dogwood. The portrait has always hung at Biltmore.

Collaborating on the interior, Hunt and Vanderbilt borrowed from four centuries to decorate the more than two hundred rooms. They created rooms in the Louis XV, Louis XVI, Jacobean, Francis I, and many other styles—a variety representative of the Victorian fascination with eclectic decoration. The interiors remain intact today with the original furnishings, many of which Hunt and Vanderbilt bought while touring Europe. Mrs. Hunt wrote in her diary of a visit they made in 1889 to the Oriental carpet warehouse of Robinson in London, where Vanderbilt bought three hundred rugs for the still unbuilt house, and then went on to Brussels to look for tapestries.[11]

The house was officially opened on Christmas Eve, 1895, with a family party that was described in both the Asheville newspapers and the *New York Times*.

Pl. X. All Souls Episcopal Church is the focal point of Biltmore village outside the gates of the estate. Hunt used the same pebble-dash-stucco walls, brick quoins, and pantile roof on all the farm buildings at Biltmore. *Smith photograph.*

Pl. XI. *Richard Morris Hunt* (1827–1895), by Sargent, 1895. Signed and dated at lower right, *John S Sargent 1895*. Oil on canvas, approximately 93 by 62 inches. The architect poses on the terrace of Biltmore, his creation. He died shortly after the picture was painted. The portrait hangs at Biltmore, as it always has.

Pl. XII. This gazebo on the bass pond is one of the many picturesque elements—bridges, buildings, waterfalls, and the like—tucked away in the park. The original drawing for the gazebo (in the Biltmore archives) describes it as a "rustic boat house." *Smith photograph.*

Pl. XIV. The native azaleas on the estate comprise one of the finest collections in the country. They were planted by Chauncey Delos Beadle, Frederick Olmsted's assistant throughout the planting in the 1890's, who remained as grounds superintendent until the 1950's. *Smith photograph.*

Pl. XIII. The Ram Branch flows through the rhododendrons on the three-mile approach road to the house. The road runs along the ravines instead of the ridges, in the midst of a dark wood full of pools, springs, and streams. *Smith photograph.*

Many details remained unfinished, but by the late 1890's George Vanderbilt's ideals were realized. In addition to the house, landscaped roads, and a five-hundred-acre landscaped park, the estate included a dairy, truck farm, chicken farm, pig farm, nurseries, and tenant farmhouses. These and other farming projects were headed by the farm manager, G. E. Weston.

Biltmore village, also designed by Hunt and Olmsted, was built in a fan shape at the entrance to the estate (see Fig. 7). It included a church (Pl. X), stores, railroad station, school, hospital, post office, recreation halls, and houses for a veterinarian, the church organist, and other estate-related workers.

Not all of Vanderbilt's plans materialized. The arboretum library which he began to assemble has disappeared; the school for horticultural and agricultural students was never established; and the arboretum itself, which Vanderbilt hoped would outshine Kew Gardens in England,[12] was never completed.

Nevertheless, Biltmore is an enduring tribute to Hunt and Olmsted, and out of friendship and gratitude for their achievement Vanderbilt brought John Singer Sargent to the house in the spring of 1895 to paint their portraits (Pl. XI, Fig. 8). He also dedicated two large stained-glass windows to them in All Souls Episcopal Church in Biltmore village.

The estate has remained relatively undisturbed, and is owned today by George and William Vanderbilt, the grandsons of the builder. It is operated for profit, making it one of the few historic houses in the country to be self-supporting. The diversity of the enterprises on the estate contributes to its profitability. In the 1920's Vanderbilt's widow deeded more than ninety thousand acres of the estate to the Department of the Interior, a tract that became the Pisgah National Forest. The forestry work started by George Vanderbilt continues, and the scenic vistas from the house are protected. Selective cutting on the remaining property continues to produce income from lumber. The truck farm and the pig and chicken farms are gone, but the dairy, owned and run by the estate, is one of the largest producers of milk in the South. Approximately two thousand dairy cows still graze on the many acres of pasture, while the bottom lands still produce corn and fodder for the herd.[13] The house and grounds, open to the public since 1930, have been made a National Historic Landmark.

Pl. XV. These tropical plants grow in one of the greenhouses that branch off the large central palm house. Additional greenhouses are used to raise bedding plants for the gardens and flowers for the house. *Smith photograph.*

Pl. XVI. Conservatories form one side of the English walled garden. The pattern beds are planted each season, and borders of perennials provide flowers for cutting and drying. *Smith photograph.*

[1] In 1900 J. Sterling Morton, who had served as secretary of agriculture from 1893 to 1897, complained that Vanderbilt had more men working on Biltmore than worked for the entire Department of Agriculture (Otis L. Graham, *The Great Campaign-Reform and War in America 1900–1928* [Englewood Cliffs, New Jersey, 1971], p. 11).

[2] In 1887 and 1888 Richard Morris Hunt designed for the farm a coachman's house, a gardener's cottage, a dairy building, a water tower, and a barn (Stapleton Dabney Gooch, "The Art and Architecture Library at Biltmore," *The American Association of Architectural Bibliographers Papers*, vol. 4, 1967, appendix B: "Buildings Executed for the Vanderbilts by Hunt").

[3] Frederick Law Olmsted Jr. to Amy Aldrick, Biltmore, July 30, 1895. A copy of the letter is in the archives at Biltmore.

[4] Mrs. William Astor's ballroom held four hundred guests. Ward McAllister, a lawyer and social leader, adopted the phrase "the four hundred" to describe the social elite of New York City.

[5] Diary of Catherine Clinton Howland Hunt, December 1894, in the Richard Morris Hunt Papers, 1828–1895, pp. 295–296. American Architectural Archives.

[6] The Biltmore Forestry School, run by Dr. Carl Alwin Schenck, a German forester, from 1898 to 1913, is now a historic site operated by the Forestry Service.

[7] Frederick Law Olmsted to Frederick Law Olmsted Jr., Brookline, Massachusetts, December 23, 1894. Frederick Law Olmsted Papers, Library of Congress, Washington, D.C.

[8] Rick Olmsted wrote in 1895: "Father and Mr. Hunt between them (Mr. V is a fairly reasonable and tractable client) planned the site and groups of buildings and the surroundings. It was on father's urging that Hunt grouped the stables with the house. . . . the extension of the house upon the other side by a long built up terrace ending in a little tea house was also his suggestion" (Frederick Law Olmsted Jr. to Amy Aldrick, Biltmore, July 30, 1895; a copy of the letter is in the Biltmore archives).

[9] Frederick Law Olmsted to William A. Stiles, Biltmore, March 10, 1895. A copy of the letter is in the Biltmore archives.

[10] Frederick Law Olmsted Jr. to a Miss Clergue, Biltmore, February 17, 1895. A copy of the letter is in the Biltmore archives.

[11] Diary of Catherine Hunt, 1889, pp. 212, 214, Hunt Papers.

[12] *New York Journal*, July 7, 1896.

[13] In addition, Biltmore Industries produces homespun fabric. It was established by Mrs. George Vanderbilt in 1901 as a craft guild to provide an outlet for the cottage industries of the mountain folk. Young boys were taught carving to produce furniture, stamp boxes, book ends, toys, and other objects. Woven baskets were made by the mountain women, and fabrics were woven on hand looms.

Chateau-sur-Mer in Newport, Rhode Island

BY JOHN A. CHEROL, *Curator of collections, Preservation Society of Newport County*

CHATEAU-SUR-MER is a formidable granite house in Newport, Rhode Island, built in 1851 and 1852 by the architect Seth Bradford for William Shepard Wetmore, formerly of New York, and his young family. Wetmore had recently retired from an extraordinary career as a banker and China Trade merchant operating between Canton, Valparaíso, London, and New York.[1] When Chateau-sur-Mer was completed on its thirty-five-acre site on the outskirts of Newport, it elicited expressions of admiration and shock from many of Newport's less affluent residents and visitors, and it made Wetmore the largest taxpayer on the city rolls. The house is situated midway along fashionable Bellevue Avenue, which was completed two years after Chateau-sur-Mer.

Wetmore enjoyed the life of a country gentleman and local grandee for several years despite the scandalous behavior of his wife, a young beauty who left her family for the thrills of Europe on the arm of one of her husband's coachmen. Wetmore bore the situation "like a hero. Instead of making a town talk, he quietly flung over it a veil of charity and silence. No one ever heard what became of his wife or his coachman."[2]

In 1862 Wetmore died, leaving the house and the bulk of his estate to his sixteen-year-old son, George Peabody Wetmore, and a generous allowance for his fourteen-year-old daughter, Annie Derby Wetmore, later Mrs. William Watts Sherman. George Peabody Wetmore graduated from Yale College in 1867 and received a law degree from Columbia in

Fig. 1. Chateau-sur-Mer, Newport, Rhode Island, built by Seth Bradford (1801–1874), 1851–1852, and completely remodeled by Richard Morris Hunt (1827–1895), 1871–1878. The photograph was taken by J. A. Williams c. 1880. *Photograph by courtesy of the Preservation Society of Newport County.*

Pl. I. The morning room, which encompasses approximately one thousand square feet, was conceived by Richard Morris Hunt in 1873 as a meeting room and auxiliary library for George Peabody Wetmore (1846–1921). Hunt is also believed to have designed the American white-oak woodwork and matching furniture in the Eastlake style. As in other rooms on the first floor, the fireplace surround is made of Minton tiles; those in this room depict the four seasons and were designed by Walter Crane (1845–1915). The interior of the fireplace is faced with Minton tile panels depicting cattails, water lilies, and insects. The walls retain their original paint, including the brick-red shadow border. The Christmas decorations here and throughout the house were inspired by nineteenth-century photographs and prints and were made by house guides who volunteered their time. The greenery comes from Chateau-sur-Mer's beautifully planted grounds. *Color photographs are by Richard Cheek.*

Pl. II. The hall, rising forty-five feet through the center of the house, was designed by Hunt and occupies the space taken up by the staircase and dining room of the house as built by Seth Bradford in 1851 and 1852. The turned and joined white-oak woodwork unifies the hall, the adjoining morning room (Pl. I), and Hunt's grand staircase (Pl.VII). On the first floor the stippled Pompeian-red walls are complemented by English stamped-velvet portières and furniture upholstered in matching fabric. The ceiling is subtly painted to resemble woven matting and is bordered with gold leaf. The second and third floors are both hung with wallpaper simulating tapestry, and have similarly frescoed ceilings representing trellises and grapevines. The stained-glass skylight was originally backlit by sixty gas jets.

1869.[3] Soon thereafter he seems to have indulged in a shopping spree in New York City, during which he purchased two sets of furniture. Léon Marcotte, who is believed to have supplied Wetmore's father with furniture for Chateau-sur-Mer more than a decade earlier (see Pl. V), provided one of the suites, which is signed by him and is decorated with Annie Wetmore's monogram.[4] He may well have provided the second suite, for it is very similar to the first (see Pl. X).

In December 1869 George Peabody Wetmore married Edith Keteltas, a member of a prominent New York and Newport family. The following year he retained Richard Morris Hunt to enlarge Chateau-sur-Mer, and he and his wife went on an extended European honeymoon while Hunt worked on the house. Except for intermittent visits to Newport in the mid-1870's the Wetmores spent almost the entire decade in Europe. They seem to have stayed principally in England, where they apparently spent much of their time shopping for furnishings in the latest style. The arts and crafts style, which was flourishing in the hands of William Morris and William Burges, was England's most avant-garde at the time, and the Wetmores purchased many of Morris' and Burges' wallpapers, encaustic tiles, hardware, fabrics, custom-made furniture, and other furnishings. They also ordered some of the considerably more flamboyant Renaissance revival work of Luigi Frullini of Florence (see Pls. III and VI).

The Wetmores returned to Newport in 1880 to a very different, much enlarged and redecorated house (Fig. 1). Hunt's extensive structural work on Chateau-sur-Mer had totally altered the plan of the

Pl. III. The carved woodwork of the walls and ceiling, the bookcases, and the floor in the library were made by Luigi Frullini (1839–1897) of Florence and installed in 1877 and 1878 in the room built by Hunt (George P. Wetmore and Luigi Frullini's correspondence, in the collection of the Preservation Society of Newport County). Frullini was also responsible for the library table and a monumental built-in desk (not visible). The marquetry floor is made up of ten varieties of wood and is said to be a copy of a floor in the Hermitage in Leningrad. The portrait above the fireplace is of George Peabody (1795–1869), the international banker, financier, and philanthropist who was William Shepard Wetmore's business partner and for whom Wetmore named his son George Peabody Wetmore.

Pl. IV. This was the main entrance hall until Hunt moved the front door to the north side of the house in the 1870's. In 1914 what had been a doorway opening to the west, at the far end of this photograph, was transformed into a windowed bay by John Russell Pope (1874–1937). The mahogany wainscoting and trim appear to survive from 1852, while the elaborate gold-leafed ceiling with stenciled and painted decoration in the Japanese taste dates from 1877. On April 2 of that year the *New York Times* reported that Wetmore's "principle rooms were being handsomely frescoed and otherwise decorated." The tufted sofas are original to the hall. The marble *Dying Gaul*, by Benjamin Paul Akers (1825–1861), was commissioned by Edward LeRoy King for the Italianate villa in Newport that Richard Upjohn designed for him in 1845.

Pl. V. The ballroom was called the gold salon by the Wetmore family. It is the only room to survive reasonably unchanged from its appearance in 1852. According to family tradition, the room was decorated and furnished by the New York firm Ringuet Le Prince and Marcotte. The ebonized chairs and sofas visible in this photograph, which survive from four matching suites of furniture originally in the room, differ only in the ormolu mounts from pieces attributed to Ringuet Le Prince and Marcotte that belonged to the John Taylor Johnstons of New York (see *19th-Century America, Furniture and other Decorative Arts* [Metropolitan Museum of Art, 1970], No. 152). They are also similar to pieces made by Marcotte for the James Browns, also of New York (see William Seale, *The Tasteful Interlude—American Interiors Through the Camera's Eye, 1860–1917* [New York, 1975], p. 42). The huge mirrors, believed to have been made in New York, are said to have been exhibited at the Crystal Palace Exposition in New York in 1853. The walls are subtly shaded, using seven tones of gray paint, and are highlighted with gold leaf. The chandeliers are thought to have been made by Cornelius and Baker of Philadelphia c. 1850. They were converted from gas to electricity sometime between 1880, when the electrification of the house began, and the 1930's, when it was completed. The Christmas tree is decorated with handmade ornaments. The door at the right leads to the Louis XV Salon, decorated in 1903 by Ogden Codman Jr. (1863–1951) as a setting for Edith Keteltas Wetmore's most important pieces of eighteenth-century French furniture, porcelain, and paintings (see ANTIQUES for September 1980, p. 497, Pl. XI).

house, which was now centered around a soaring three-story hall (see Pl. II). Another major feature of the new plan was the magnificent staircase (Pl. VII), which rises four flights into the tower Hunt added to the north side of the house. The only first-floor room to remain unchanged from the 1852 house was the gold salon, later called the ballroom (Pl. V).

During the 1880's the Wetmores, their four children, and the necessary entourage of nannies, nurses, and the like made Chateau-sur-Mer not only their summer home, but one of their major year-round houses as well. They also kept residences in Washington, D. C., and New York City and made frequent trips to London and Paris. George Peabody Wetmore was made a presidential elector in 1880 and 1884, and between 1885 and 1887 he was governor of Rhode Island.[5] In the 1890's the house was used only in the summer, for the family began to spend more time in Washington and New York after Wetmore was elected to the United States Senate in 1894.[6]

Wetmore died on September 11, 1921, and since his wife was ill, the supervision of the house fell to his two daughters, Maude and Edith Wetmore.[7] They maintained the property much as their parents had, except that they radically modernized some of the bedrooms, bathrooms, dressing rooms, and one of the second-floor sitting rooms. Most notably, they painted over the elaborate painted, gilded, and stenciled ceiling in Mrs. Wetmore's bedroom, removed the wallpaper of the 1870's, and painted the walls and woodwork in the room a uniform gray-beige.

The last of the Wetmores, Edith, died in 1966 at the age of ninety-five. After much litigation the Preservation Society of Newport County acquired Chateau-sur-Mer. The contents of the house were put up for sale,[8] and a number of key pieces of furniture were purchased by friends of the Preservation Society, who subsequently donated them to the Society. In the past five years the Society has tried to reintroduce some of the original vigor to the interiors, particularly by restoring the important decorative schemes inspired by the aesthetic movement that had been erased during the modernization of the Misses Wetmore. The discovery of the painted ceiling in Mrs. Wetmore's bedroom, beautifully intact beneath the calcimine paint, spurred restoration of that room in 1977 (Pl. VIII). More recently, the northwest bedroom, called the Butternut Room because the furniture and trim in it are made of that light-color hardwood, has been restored (Pl. X).

Since 1975, during the Christmas season the Preservation Society of Newport County has decorated Chateau-sur-Mer in the style in the 1880's and opened it to the public. The interior is hung with hundreds of yards of fresh laurel roping and quantities of evergreen boughs, all grown on the grounds of the estate. A sixteen-foot-tall live Christmas tree decked with ribbons, bows, packages, candies, paper fans, glass beads, and candles dominates the ballroom. The ornate dining room is sumptuously set for a festive dinner using antique porcelain, glass, and silver and Wetmore family linens. The whole evokes the spirit of merry Christmases past.

Pl. VI. The dining room, like the library, was created by Frullini of Florence and installed in 1877 and 1878. The Circassian-walnut ceiling is carved with grape clusters, vines, and elaborate moldings that frame a central painting. The walls are covered with the same tooled, gilded, and painted leather that upholsters the chairs and matching footrests. The burl-walnut paneling has carved borders of fruit and flowers. The sideboard is embellished with a Minton plaque, as is an elaborate mantel-cum-serving cabinet on the opposite wall. The silver flatware, in the English King pattern, was made by Tiffany and Company c. 1900. The centerpiece, flanked by orchids and asparagus fern, is part of a monumental silver *surtout-de-table* depicting the Judgment of Paris that was made by Paul Storr (1771–1844) of London in 1822. The Irish linen bears the Wetmore family's elaborate crest; the napkins are folded according to instructions in Isabella Beeton's *Book of Household Management* of 1893.

[1] Walter Barrett, *Old Merchants of New York City* (New York, 1872), vol. 2, part 1, p. 293.

[2] *Ibid.*, p. 299.

[3] *History of Newport County Rhode Island*, ed. Richard M. Bayles (New York, 1888), p. 610.

[4] A washstand from the suite is inscribed *George P. Wetmore, Esq., Newport, RI L. Marcotte, New York 1869.* The washstand is in a private collection. Other pieces from the set are in Chateau-sur-Mer.

[5] Bayles, *History of Newport County*, p. 610.

[6] Mrs. John King Van Rensselaer, *Newport Our Social Capital* (Philadelphia and London, 1905), p. 52. Wetmore was a senator from 1894 until 1907 and again from 1908 to 1913.

[7] Last Will and Testament of George P. Wetmore, December 17, 1918, City of Newport Record of Probate, Book 83, p. 94; Newport City Hall, Newport, Rhode Island.

[8] *Furniture, Porcelain, Silver and other works of Art at Chateau-sur-Mer, Newport residence of the late Edith M. K. Wetmore and Maude A. K. Wetmore* (Parke-Bernet Galleries, sale no. 2888, 1969).

Pl. VII. View of the main staircase from the first landing. This staircase is the most spectacular of Richard Morris Hunt's designs for Chateau-sur-Mer. The way is lit by bronze *torchères* on the upper levels, while on the first floor, gilt-trimmed bronze figures of a Japanese maiden and a geisha hold blossoming branches of cherry which incorporate light bulbs. Modeled by Jean Baptiste Claude Eugène Guillaume, these two figures were cast at Barbidiene Foundries in Paris c. 1890 and were acquired by the Wetmores when they were exhibited at the Louisiana Purchase Exposition in St. Louis in 1904.

Pl. VIII. The ceiling in Edith Keteltas Wetmore's bedroom, originally elaborately painted in delicate pastels and gilded, was later covered by layers of calcimine paint. When the room was restored in 1977 the overpainting was carefully removed to reveal the original decoration. The wallpaper and frieze are reproductions after samples of the originals deposited at the Cooper-Hewitt Museum by Edith and Maude Wetmore in the early part of this century. The original frieze and wallpaper are believed to have been made in France c. 1875. The rosewood mantel carved with Japanese motifs was made by Gregory and Company of Regent Street, London, in 1876. The bed and wardrobe, part of the original suite of furniture in this room, were acquired by the Philadelphia Museum of Art when the contents of the house were auctioned in 1969. They are now on loan to the Preservation Society of Newport County. Most of the upholstered furniture in this room is original to the house, as are the Belgian-lace curtains. The portrait on the easel beside the fireplace is of George Peabody Wetmore and was painted by his cousin Julian Story (1850–1919) in 1892. The carpet is a mid-nineteenth-century Aubusson.

Pl. IX. George Peabody Wetmore's bedroom was untouched by the Misses Wetmore during their redecorating campaign and thus survives as an important example of an interior in the style of the English aesthetic movement. The ceiling is painted and stenciled to complement the wallpaper. The frieze paper was designed by William Morris (1834–1896), as was the flocked Willow-pattern paper in the bed alcove. The bed is part of a four-piece suite of red-stained and ebonized mahogany furniture made by Gregory and Company in 1876. The elaborate matching chimney breast in the room (not visible in this photograph) was also made by Gregory and Company.

Pl. X. The seventeen-piece suite of butternut furniture in the Butternut Room is believed to be the second set of furniture George Peabody Wetmore ordered from Léon Marcotte in 1869. It bears Wetmore's monogram. The armchair to the left of the fireplace, upholstered with a Sehna kilim carpet, is original to the house. The elaborate ceiling was never painted over, but it did require extensive restoration. The wallpaper was reproduced from remnants of the original French paper of c. 1872 that were found on the walls of the room and from documents deposited in the Cooper-Hewitt Museum. The griffin frieze was designed by William Burges (1827–1881) and first appeared in trade catalogues in 1872. The wool and lame flame-stitch draperies are original to the room. The bedspread was embroidered in Italy in the nineteenth century. The biscuit-porcelain figure of Hamlet on the linen press was modeled by John Rogers (1829–1904). On the wall behind it are hand-tinted photographs taken by Mathew B. Brady (c. 1823–1896) of New York. The clock and matching candelabra on the mantel were made by Tiffany and Company in 1875; the art-pottery vases on the mantel were made by John Bennett (w. in New York 1876–1882) in 1880 (left) and 1882 (right). Above the mantel hangs *Homage paid to Charles V by the Knights of the Golden Fleece*, painted by Albrecht Frans Lievin De Vriendt (1843–1900) c. 1875.

Villa Finale: the San Antonio residence of Walter Nold Mathis

BY ELISABETH DONAGHY GARRETT

Pl. I. Villa Finale, 401 King William Street, San Antonio, Texas, was begun in 1876 and enlarged later in the nineteenth century. The house was built for Russell C. Norton and was subsequently owned by the rancher Edwin Polk and the celebrated trail boss and cattleman Ike T. Pryor. The present owner, Walter Nold Mathis, acquired the house, which is also known as the Norton-Polk-Mathis house, in 1967. *Photographs are by Helga Photo Studio.*

THE BRILLIANT San Antonio sunshine accents the sculptural robustness achieved by the German stonemasons who in 1876 began to build the Italianate house now known as Villa Finale for the hardware merchant Russell C. Norton. The bold opulence of the mansion suggests something of the prosperity which accompanied the arrival of the railroad in San Antonio in the late 1870's. Attesting to the affluence of their owners, more than twenty handsome stone Victorian houses and many fine wooden ones were built near Villa Finale in the last quarter of the nineteenth century.[1]

Pl. II.   The center hall divides the library (Pls. III, IV) and dining room (Pls. VIII, IX and Fig. 4) on the south from the large double parlor on the north (Pls. V-VII and Fig. 3). The restored gold stenciled border above the chair rail continues around the double parlor and up the stair well. The equestrian bronzes were both modeled by Antoine Louis Barye (1795–1875) in the 1840's. The one on the left, entitled *The Young Bonaparte*, is stamped on the base, BARYE 2; the one on the right, entitled *Duke of Orléans*, is stamped BARYE 4. Barye also made the gilt-bronze candelabra of 1840, which stand on elaborate ebony, bird's-eye-maple, and gilt-bronze pedestals. They flank a painted and gilded side table and mirror made in Italy in the eighteenth century. The views of Venice were painted by a member of the school of Antonio Canaletto (1697–1768). The benches are English. On the floor is a South Persian tribal rug.

The once-polished neighborhood, five minutes from downtown San Antonio, had greatly deteriorated by the time Walter Nold Mathis purchased Villa Finale in 1967. Mr. Mathis' subsequent restoration of the house served as the catalyst for the historic preservation movement in the area, and under his leadership a number of other houses on King William Street and the surrounding blocks have been restored. In 1968 the city of San Antonio made the section a historic district and it is listed on the National Register of Historic Places.

Fig. 1. The elaborate front door was carved in England specifically for the house c. 1876. The ornate bronze hardware is typical of that discovered under layers of paint on doors and windows throughout the house. The blue and brown porch tiles are original (see also p. 143).

Fig. 2. The Empire pier table and convex gilded mirror in the center hall are Continental. On the chest at the corner of the stair is a pair of Argand lamps made early in the nineteenth century by J. and I. Cox of New York City. The oval stained-glass window above the stair landing is one of nine restored for the present owner.

The restoration of the Mathis house took a year. The limestone of which it is built—quarried near Fredericksburg, Texas—was steam cleaned to remove layers of paint from the intricately carved detailing of the capitals and friezes. The shaped tin shingles on the tower roof were scraped down and missing ones were replaced. The few remaining original cypress shutters were repaired and replicas were made to replace those that had been destroyed. A wrought-iron gazebo that had once stood in the formal garden on the south side of the house was rebuilt and is illustrated on p. 143.

Pl. III. The fireplace in the library is one of eight in the house, all of which have been restored. On the mantel are a pair of malachite urns made c. 1780 by the Russian sculptor Michel Kozlovsky (1753–1802) and two English bronze spill vases of c. 1810. The spills in the vases were reproduced from a single original found in one of them. The eighteenth-century mirror is French. On the bookshelves and the table at the left is an important collection of French bronzes by Isidore Jules Bonheur (1827–1901), Pierre Jules Mène (1810–1879), and Antoine Louis Barye. The carpet is a Kashan.

Pl. IV. Russian, Greek, Spanish, and Spanish colonial icons hang in this corner of the library. The lamp is made from a Spanish colonial figure of Saint Anthony of Padua, the patron saint of San Antonio. On the table at the right is a collection of snuffboxes.

Pl. VI. A collection of prints relating to Napoleon adorns this wall of the double parlor. The sofa and side chair are part of the same set as the furniture shown in Pl. V.

Pl. V. The detailed plasterwork in the north, double, parlor is notable. The French Empire writing table was made *en suite* with the six side chairs, four armchairs, two barrel-back chairs, one sofa, and one stool in the room (see also Pl. VI and Fig. 3). On the writing table are silver, bronze, ivory, and wooden figures of Napoleon. The bronze bust of Napoleon as a general, at the extreme right, is signed and dated 1805 by the Italian sculptor Petronio Nannini (d. 1806). Opposite it, on the left side of the room, is a bronze of Napoleon as first consul by the French sculptor and painter Antoine Denis Chaudet (1763–1810). Early nineteenth-century Sèvres vases stand on a pair of encoignures which are stamped LESAGE, RUE GRANGE BATELIERE No 2 A PARIS. Antoine Nicolas Lesage (1784–1841) was the director of Union des arts, an exclusive furniture store in Paris in the nineteenth century.

Inside, plasterwork and woodwork were repaired and restored, and the vivacious gold-stenciled border above the chair rail in the downstairs hall and double parlor was returned to its original brilliance (see Pls. II, V-VII, and Fig. 2). Mr. Mathis has furnished the house with Continental art, including French bronzes and objects associated with Napoleon; family furnishings; and objects made in Texas.

In 1877 Harriet Prescott Spofford described the mansions along King William Street in terms that could easily be applied to Villa Finale today: ". . . you will find, behind broad porches, lofty rooms with polished floors and rugs, books and pictures and vases and costly furniture. . . ."[2] The handsome elegance of Villa Finale evokes the halcyon days of King William Street at the end of the nineteenth century, but its easy elegance belies the labor and dedication required to restore the house to its early state.

---

[1] See ANTIQUES for September 1975, pp. 447-455.

[2] "San Antonio de Bexar," *Harper's New Monthly Magazine,* November 1877; quoted in Cecilia Steinfeldt, *San Antonio Was: Seen Through a Magic Lantern* (San Antonio, 1978), p. 170.

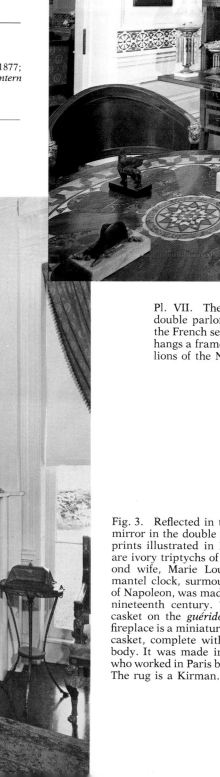

Pl. VII. The marble-topped table in the double parlor was made in Europe. Above the French secretary of the Louis XVI period hangs a framed collection of intaglio medallions of the Napoleonic period.

Fig. 3. Reflected in the French overmantel mirror in the double parlor is the cluster of prints illustrated in Pl. VI. On the mantel are ivory triptychs of Napoleon and his second wife, Marie Louise (1791–1847). The mantel clock, surmounted by a cast figure of Napoleon, was made in Lyons in the early nineteenth century. The bronze and gold casket on the *guéridon* to the right of the fireplace is a miniature replica of Napoleon's casket, complete with a removable bronze body. It was made in 1840 by E. Quesnel, who worked in Paris between 1811 and 1847. The rug is a Kirman.

Fig. 4. A painting of St. Cecilia in the manner of Michelangelo Merisi da Caravaggio (1573–1610) hangs in the dining room. The silver tea service on the English side table beneath the painting is by the firm of Henry Ball, Erastus O. Tompkins, and William Black of New York City (w. together 1839–1851). The mahogany cellaret beneath the table is English.

Pl. VIII. The English chandelier, French overmantel mirror, and American mahogany chairs lend a cosmopolitan air to the dining room. On the dining table are four silver salts representing the Four Continents which bear the mark used by the London silversmith Robert Garrard II (1793–1881) between 1822 and 1847. The silver-gilt epergne on a mirrored plateau and the matching standing fruit bowl (one of a pair) are decorated with silver sphinxes and camels. They were made in England to commemorate the opening of the Suez Canal in 1869. Transfer-printed ware from the Texian Campaigne series by the Mersey Pottery of Burslem, Staffordshire, hangs on the far wall.

Pl. IX. Mr. Mathis' silver collection includes the English goblets shown here. The silver pitchers were made by John Kitts and Company of Louisville, Kentucky, which was in business from 1859 until 1863, when the name was changed to Kitts and Werne. The handsome eighteenth-century mahogany and satinwood knife cases are English.

Fig. 5. The second-floor south sitting room contains much family furniture and memorabilia, including an early Victrola. The fine pocket watch on the table in the foreground was decorated in four colors of gold by the San Antonio silversmith Samuel Bell (w. c. 1848–1860), an ancestor of Mr. Mathis. The decoration on the gas chandelier (now wired for electricity), made in New York c. 1840, includes Indians armed with bows.

Fig. 6. The circular stair in the north sitting room on the second floor leads to a bedroom above. The gilded cornices above the windows came from a plantation house on the Mississippi River. Mr. Mathis purchased the rococo revival settee and chairs in New Orleans. The pedestal table was made in Texas c. 1850. The settee in the foreground is French; the shaving stand at the right is Continental. See also Pl. X.

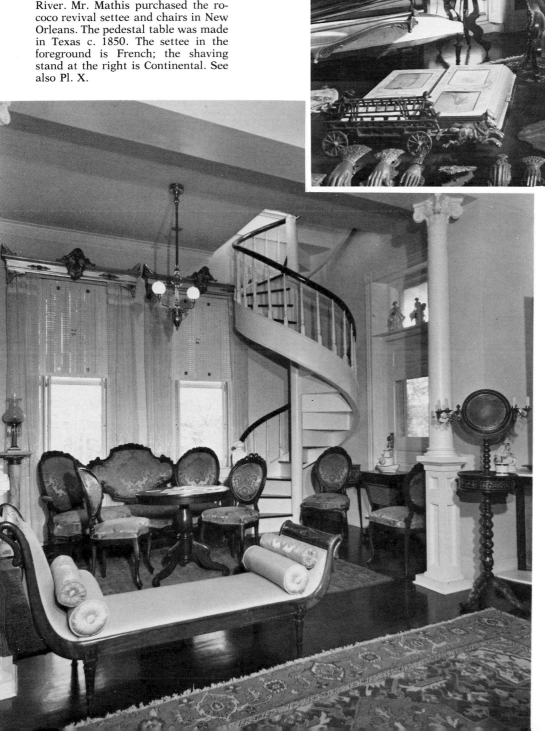

Pl. X. At the other end of the sitting room shown in Fig. 6 is an Empire mahogany sleigh bed. The late nineteenth-century washstand is a copy of the one Empress Joséphine used at Malmaison.

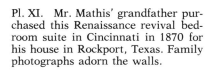

Pl. XI. Mr. Mathis' grandfather purchased this Renaissance revival bedroom suite in Cincinnati in 1870 for his house in Rockport, Texas. Family photographs adorn the walls.

Fig. 7. Currier and Ives lithographs of the Mexican War adorn the walls of this second-floor bedroom. The nineteenth-century bed, stamped LEE, was made in New Orleans. The quilt was sewed by Mr. Mathis' paternal grandmother, Mary Jane Nold Mathis, of Rockport. The walnut chest with dressing mirror was made in Texas c. 1850.

Fig. 8. Texas' early days are recalled in this study on the second floor by the Texas-made furniture, pottery, and revolvers, and paintings of the Southwest by Theodore Gentilz (c. 1820–1906). The stove, patented in 1852, is one of four wood-burning stoves used in the house.

Pl. XII. American, English, and Continental pewter is displayed in a small room adjoining the kitchen. The late nineteenth-century walnut table is from New Braunfels, Texas; the pewter candlesticks on it are Continental.

Fig. 9. A Rhine maiden offers a cup of wine from the rustic German chandelier in the small room next to the kitchen (see also Pl. XII). The Old World is also recalled by the Spanish altar chest under the window, the Germanic nineteenth-century stove, the turned French cupboard at the left, and the Dutch, French, and English paintings.

Pl. XIII. The upstairs kitchen captures the good fun Walter Mathis had restoring and furnishing his house. The art-glass chandelier was in the house when he bought it. The Southern pine cupboard at the left, c. 1878, was salvaged from the Sullivan house, which once stood on Broadway in San Antonio. Inside the cupboard are Sèvres dinner and tea services bearing the monogram of Napoleon III and the date 1858. The deep dish and jar on the Texas magnolia-wood table of c. 1850 are part of Mr. Mathis' collection of Meyer pottery. The oak chairs came from La Quinta, the headquarters of the Taft Ranch in Gregory, Texas. The Enterprise Manufacturing Company of Philadelphia made the large coffee mill that stands in front of the refrigerator. Early kitchen tools complement the colorful array of spices, candies, and dried foods stored in apothecary jars. The kitchen epitomizes the Southern hospitality remembered by Tulitas Wulff Jamieson, who wrote of her girlhood near King William Street, "There were cakes so light they had to be held down with inch thick icings, rolls that vanished in your mouth like a puff of smoke, great roasts of beef with thick delicious gravy, chicken cooked in a dozen ways, home-made bread that tasted better than any bakery ever smelled, *tortes* smothered in whipped cream" (quoted in Cecilia Steinfeldt, *San Antonio Was: Seen Through a Magic Lantern* [San Antonio, 1978], p. 172).

Fig. 10. The basement kitchen, filled with early kitchen equipment, is still used for cooking on special occasions. The pottery butter churn next to the door is one of many objects in the house made by the Meyer Pottery in Atascosa County, Texas. The stove partly visible at the right is marked LEIBRANDT & MCDOWELL STOVE CO. PHILADELPHIA AND BALTIMORE.

Facing page:
Pl. XIV. Gazebo in the garden of Villa Finale, San Antonio, Texas.

Fig. 11. In this room in the basement a poker table from the Kendall Inn in Boerne, Texas, chairs from the old San Antonio Casino Club, and a domino table from a New Braunfels tavern conjure up the leisure pastimes of an earlier day in Texas. The domino table is marked E. PUCKTA PAT. FEB. 15 1881. Decorating the back wall is collection of beer mugs, including small ladies' glasses, from San Antonio's Pearl Brewery. In the cupboard are pieces of Staffordshire ware from the Texian Campaigne series (see also Pl. VIII).

The early interiors of Carrère and Hastings

BY CHANNING BLAKE

JOHN MERVEN CARRERE (1858-1911) and Thomas Hastings (1860-1929) met in 1882 as students at the Ecole des Beaux-Arts in Paris, and from 1883 to 1885 worked as draftsmen for McKim, Mead and White in New York. When Henry M. Flagler approached them in 1885 to design the Ponce de Leon Hotel in St. Augustine, Florida, as part of the development of what he called "the American Riviera," the two young men established a firm of their own that flourished until 1929. Carrère, an impetuous but methodical man, ran the business and dealt with the clients. Hastings, a warm and generous person, designed the buildings.

Amid the differing architectural philosophies of the last two decades of the nineteenth century, Carrère and Hastings were the leading proponents of the Beaux-Arts, or "modern French," style. Among their principles were to resolve the practical problems of a commission by means of a well-conceived plan and to incorporate elements of the interior into the façade. As Hastings wrote in later years, a building had to operate efficiently and economically to be considered successful.[1] In complicated building programs such as the New Theatre on Central Park West (now demolished) the architects were willing to sacrifice the monumental gran-

Fig. 1. Entrance hall of the Ponce de Leon Hotel, St. Augustine, Florida, built 1885-1887, c. 1900. *Photograph by courtesy of the Henry Morrison Flagler Museum.*

deur of the façade to the inner workings of the structure.[2] By contrast, McKim, Mead and White had a breathtaking ability to create handsome façades for clubs, residences, and public buildings. Carrère and Hastings practiced a variety of French styles, including the seventeenth-century brick-and-limestone idiom for country houses, the Louis XVI style for town houses (most notably the Henry Frick mansion in New York), and the "modern French" style for their public buildings. By 1900 many of their ideas and designs had found significant recognition in public competitions, and the firm was considered the equal of the more classically oriented McKim, Mead and White. Carrère and Hastings' clients were conservative, wealthy bankers, lawyers, industrialists, and railroad men, and later the United States government, for the House and Senate Office Buildings (1905-1909) in Washington and the National Amphitheatre (1915-1920) in Arlington.

The Ponce de Leon Hotel (1885-1887) demonstrated Carrère and Hastings' ability to handle a complex building. The plan consisted of a central axis composed of large geometric shapes—a square front courtyard, an octagonal entrance hall (Fig. 1) and a rectangular dining room (Fig. 2) flanked by semicircular dining areas. The salon (Fig. 3), a series of three parallel rectangles, terminated a cross axis that ran through the entrance hall. The building, in the "Spanish Renaissance" style, was built in cast concrete with molded terra-cotta details. Throughout the interiors the architects indulged a late Victorian taste for abrupt juxtapositions of forms, vivid contrasts of materials, and idiosyncratic reinterpretations of Renaissance ornament. The carved-wood and molded plaster ornament and the murals were fully developed, but they failed to achieve a stylistic unity in each room. The architects, caught up in what Hastings later termed "the enthusiasms of youth,"[3] made little attempt to harmonize materials and decorative motifs or impose a logical progression on the structural elements. Thus, for example, the three levels of the entrance hall were not well related visually. The vertical emphasis of the four-sided caryatids was diluted by the arcades of the second level, and finally abandoned in the third-floor drum. The dining room possessed greater coherence because of the grandeur of the central vault and the use of Corinthian columns around the perimeter. The same decorative exuberance and broad handling of the Renaissance style and varied materials is evident in the hall at William Rockefeller's residence in Tarrytown, which Carrère and Hastings installed in 1888 (Fig. 4).

In the architects' earliest interiors we find two stylistic tendencies which remain evident throughout their work. First, Hastings as a designer was extremely fond of elegant ornament. He enjoyed penciling in candelabra, cartouches, festoons, rinceaux, and shells while avoiding the misapplied historic motifs that often characterized the work of other American graduates of the Ecole des Beaux-Arts. It is easy to understand his attraction to Pinturrichio's ceilings for the Borgia Apartments in the Vatican which he recreated on the ceiling of the Ponce Hotel dining room. In the 1890's Hastings began to restrain his use of ornament, as is evident in the ladies' lounge (Fig. 6) of the Jefferson Hotel (1893-

1895) in Richmond, Virginia. And after 1900, when the trend was toward simpler architectural styles, he had to confine his ornamental details to modest wall panels.

The second consistent stylistic feature of Carrère and Hastings' work was a preference for distinctly flat wall treatment. Cornices projected less than their historic prototypes, pilasters seemed almost to sink into the walls, and carved or cast ornament had linear rather than sculptural

Fig. 2. Dining room of the Ponce de Leon Hotel, c. 1900. *Flagler Museum photograph.*

Fig. 3. Salon of the Ponce de Leon Hotel, c. 1900. *Flagler Museum photograph.*

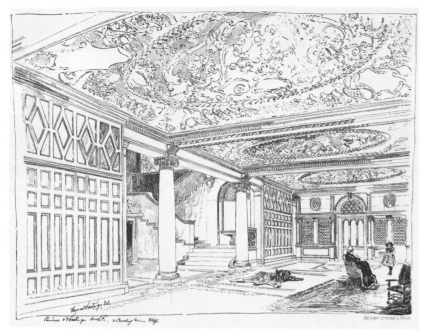

Fig. 4. Hall at Rockwood Hall, Tarrytown, New York, redecorated by Carrère and Hastings for William Rockefeller in 1888. The house was demolished in the 1930's. The illustration is from *American Architect and Building News*, August 4, 1888, Pl. 658.

impact. The paneling and molded ceilings of the hall in the Rockefeller house (Fig. 4) are set within a grid of pilasters and entablatures. The columns and coffering of the Jefferson Hotel's ladies' lounge (Fig. 6) lose their three-dimensional impact and are subordinated to the wall surfaces. In later years as the architects minimized the use

Fig. 5. Dining room of the Jefferson Hotel, Richmond, Virginia, built 1893-1895. This room was destroyed by fire in 1905. *Photograph by courtesy of the Valentine Museum.*

of ornament they relied more and more upon the subtle play of large plane surfaces (see Fig. 9).

Beginning in the middle of the 1890's the firm designed a series of stylish Edwardian country houses, an area of architectural practice which they dominated until 1915. The first of these was a summer house at the end of Indian Harbor Point, Greenwich, Connecticut, built for the investment banker E. C. Benedict. It was an L-shape building with the entrance hall (Fig. 7) at the intersection of the axes, the dining room straight ahead along the main axis, and the drawing room (Fig. 8) off the right of the entrance hall. In these interiors we see a simplification of Carrère and Hastings' decorative style and a codification of the architectural syntax that they adhered to in most of the firm's residential commissions for the next thirty years. Rooms became simple squares or rectangles arranged around a central organizing element, the hall. The use of columns and entablatures was confined to the hall, while the other rooms were notable for the flatness of their wall treatment. In the drawing room of the Benedict house, for example, the walls were reduced to a flat grid of horizontals and verticals with the intervening spaces upholstered in damask or filled with carved panels in the Louis XVI style. Only the overmantel extended into the clearly defined space. Other decorations such as the furniture, porcelain, and the pictures do not intrude upon the architectural framework.

The flatness of wall treatment is refined to an unusual degree at Blairsden, the sumptuous country estate of C. Ledyard Blair, a railroad and investment magnate, built between 1898 and 1903 at Peapack, New Jersey. In the limestone hall (Fig. 9) and the fifty-four by twenty-five-foot drawing room (Fig. 10) the decorative detail on the walls is reduced to a minimum. The two fireplaces in the drawing

Fig. 6. Ladies' lounge of the Jefferson Hotel. *Valentine Museum photograph.*

Fig. 7. Entrance hall of the E. C. Benedict house, Greenwich, Connecticut, built 1895-1896. The interiors are now demolished. *Photograph by courtesy of the Museum of the City of New York.*

Fig. 8. Drawing room of the Benedict house. *Museum of the City of New York photograph.*

room push forward to establish the two main sitting areas, but the Ionic volutes hardly project from the wall plane.

In a few cases the architects had to submit to the wishes of strong-willed clients and produce rooms in eighteenth-century styles. For his large house in Lenox, Massachusetts, Giraud Foster had them design a Louis XIV dining room, a Régence library, and a rococo drawing room. The *Architectural Review* noted the incongruity of the rooms in a house set in the Berkshires, and called the treatment "very sumptuous . . . but also so correct in its Frenchiness, that it gives almost the idea of an unusually perfect stage setting."[4]

Mrs. Richard Townsend of Washington, D. C., also made certain demands when she called upon the architects to alter and enlarge an 1870's mansion as a setting for her large and lavish entertainments. The façade she wanted "to look like the Petit Trianon."[5] The reception rooms were arranged to facilitate the circulation of the guests, and were decorated for large-scale effects. In the sitting room (Fig. 11), for example, the carved and composition ornament surges over the cornice and ceiling more freely than in other contemporary rooms designed by the firm.

For the entrance hall (Fig. 12) of his mansion, Whitehall, in Palm Beach, Henry Flagler forced the architects to place the ceiling eight feet lower than they had intended, for he claimed that his was "a house to be lived in,"[6] rather than a palace. For his ballroom (Fig. 13), Flagler had Carrère and Hastings reproduce the one they had designed

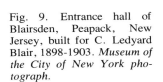

Fig. 9. Entrance hall of Blairsden, Peapack, New Jersey, built for C. Ledyard Blair, 1898-1903. *Museum of the City of New York photograph.*

Fig. 10. Drawing room of Blairsden. *Museum of the City of New York photograph.*

Fig. 11. Sitting room at the house of Mrs. Richard Townsend, 2121 Massachusetts Avenue, Washington, D. C., enlarged and redecorated by Carrère and Hastings 1898-1901. *Photograph by courtesy of the Library of Congress.*

Fig. 12. Entrance hall of White-hall, Palm Beach, Florida, built for Henry Flagler, 1900-1902. *Flagler Museum photograph.*

for his friend Mrs. Townsend. In doing so the architects kept the same wall elevation and ceiling height but lengthened the room considerably so that the ceiling has five, not three, coffers.

The John Henry Hammond house at 9 East 91st Street in New York shows Carrère and Hastings again working in the Louis XVI style, which was compatible with their predilection for flat surfaces and with the general evolution after 1900 toward a reduction of ornament. The style provided numerous ways of filling wall space with *boiserie*, plasterwork (see Fig. 14), fabric, tapestry, or latticework.

This was necessary as, with the exception of Henry Frick, the firm's clients did not collect works of art. Carrère and Hastings never introduced architectural fragments imported from Europe, as did their good friend Stanford White, and only in exceptional cases such as the high-ceilinged Hammond library (Fig. 15) did they resort to an arresting sculptural device such as the voluted fireplace. In general they sought the tightest control over clearly defined spaces, unbroken surfaces, and luxuriously conceived details which ensured a distinctive appearance for their Edwardian interiors.

Fig. 13. Ballroom at White-hall. *Flagler Museum photo-graph.*

150

Fig. 14. Music room of the John Henry Hammond house, 9 East 91st Street, New York City, built 1902. *Photograph by courtesy of Mrs. B. Goodman.*

[1] David Gray, *Thomas Hastings, Architect* (Boston, 1933).

[2] This was recognized in their own time. See "The Work of Messers Carrère and Hastings," in *The Architectural Record*, January 1910, p. 103.

[3] "A Letter from Thomas Hastings, F.A.I.A. Reminiscent of the Early Work of Messers Carrère and Hastings, Architects," *American Architect*, July 7, 1907, pp. 3-4. Esther McCoy (*Five California Architects*, New York, 1960, p. 5) has suggested that Bernard Maybeck, a draftsman with the firm who was in Florida during the course of construction, may have been responsible for some of the "enthusiasm" of the decorations. However, Carrère and Hastings probably retained control of the design of the Ponce interiors, their first important public interiors.

[4] *The Architectural Review*, May 1902, p. 106. The interiors of the Foster house were illustrated in *American Architect and Building News*, April 5, 1902, Pl. 1371.

[5] Commission of Fine Arts, *Massachusetts Avenue Architecture* (Washington, 1973), p. 203.

[6] Edwin LeFevre, "Conversation with Henry Morrison Flagler," *Everybody's Magazine*, November 13, 1910, p. 25.

Fig. 15. Library of the Hammond house. *Goodman photograph.*

Selected Bibliography

American Life Foundation Study Institute. *Furniture for the Victorian Home.* Comprising the abridged furniture sections from A.J. Downing, *The Architecture of Country Houses* (1850) and J.C. Loudon, *Encyclopedia of Cottage, Farm, and Villa Architecture and Furniture* (1833). Watkins Glen, N.Y.: American Life Foundation, 1978.

Butler, Joseph T. *American Antiques, 1800-1900.* New York: Bonanza, 1965.

Clark, Robert Judson. *The Arts and Crafts Movement in America, 1876-1916.* Princeton: Princeton University Press, 1972.

Cook, Clarence. *The House Beautiful.* Reprint. New York: North River Press, 1980.

Davidson, Marshall B., ed. *The American Heritage History of Antiques from the Civil War to World War I.* New York: American Heritage Publishing Co., 1969.

Downing, Andrew J. *The Architecture of Country Houses.* Reprint. New York: Dover Publications, 1969.

_____. *Victorian Cottage Residences.* Reprint. New York: Dover Publications, 1981.

Eastlake, Charles L. *Hints on Household Taste.* Reprint. New York: Dover Publications, 1969.

Garrett, Wendell D., et al. *The Arts in America: The Nineteenth Century.* New York: Charles Scribner's Sons, 1969.

Howe, Katherine S. and David D. Warren. *The Gothic Revival Style in America, 1830-70.* Houston, Texas. The Museum of Fine Arts, 1975.

Lambourne, Lionel. *Utopian Craftsmen.* Salt Lake City: Peregrine Smith, Inc., 1980.

Lockwood, Charles. *Bricks & Brownstone: The New York Row House.* New York: McGraw-Hill Book Co., 1972.

Lynes, Russell. *The Art-Makers of Nineteenth-Century America.* New York: Atheneum Publishers, 1970.

_____. *The Domesticated Americans.* New York: Harper & Row, 1957.

Lynn, Catherine. *Wallpaper in America.* New York: Norton, 1980.

Madigan, Mary Jean Smith. *Eastlake-Influenced American Furniture, 1870-1890.* Yonkers, N.Y.: Hudson River Museum, 1973.

The Metropolitan Museum of Art. *19th-Century Furniture and Other Decorative Arts.* Greenwich, Conn.: New York Graphic Society, 1970.

_____. *19th-Century American Paintings and Sculpture.* Greenwich, Conn.: New York Graphic Society, 1970.

Myers, Minor and Edgar Mayhew. *A Documentary History of American Interiors.* New York: Charles Scribner's Sons, 1980.

The Newark Museum. *Classical America 1815-1845.* Newark, 1963.

Peterson, Harold. *American Interiors.* New York: Charles Scribner's Sons, 1971.

Schwartz, Marvin D., et al. *The Furniture of John Henry Belter and the Rococo Revival.* New York: Elsevier-Dutton Publishing Co., 1981.

Seale, William. *Recreating the Historic House Interior.* Nashville, Tenn.: American Association for State and Local History, 1979.

Stillinger, Elizabeth. *The Antiquers.* New York: Alfred A. Knopf, 1980.

About the Contributors

Channing Blake completed graduate studies in architectural preservation at Columbia University and has recently published a book on the work of Carrère and Hastings.

Susanne Brendel-Pandich is the curator of Biltmore, Asheville, North Carolina.

John A. Cherol is the Registrar of the Preservation Society of Newport, Rhode Island.

Thomas D. Clark is a professor of history and is the author of numerous books and articles on midwestern and southern themes.

Wilson H. Faude is the Executive Director of the Old State House in Hartford, Connecticut.

Elisabeth Donaghy Garret is the former curator of the DAR Museum in Washington, D.C., and is the author of the companion book, *The Antiques Book of American Interiors: Colonial and Federal Styles.* She is also a frequent contributor to *The Magazine Antiques* and is married to *Antiques* publisher, Wendell Garret.

Peter L. Goss is associated with the Graduate School of Architecture of the University of Utah and is a member of the Society of Architectural Historians.

Eleanor H. Gustafson is an assistant editor for *The Magazine Antiques.*

Margaret Rose Ingate appraises fine arts and home furnishings and is a member of the Appraisers Association of America.

David M. Kahn is the former curator of the Theodore Roosevelt Birthplace and Grant's Tomb in New York City.

Margaret N. Keyes is the director of Old Capitol in Iowa City and is a professor of home economics at the University of Iowa.

Betsy Knight, a free-lance writer in the decorative arts and fine arts, has been on the staff of the Smithsonian Institution and the Bayou Bend Collection in Houston.

Henry W. Krotzer is a restoration architect based in New Orleans.

Kathleen Nelson Taggart is the research historian for the John Wornall House in Kansas City; she is married to Ross Taggart, Director of the William Rockhill Nelson Gallery and Atkins Museum of Fine Arts in Kansas City.

Index